Praise for *In*

"A tremendous resource, amalgamating that is presented in a concise, easy to read format." – Alan H. Aronson, Shareholder, Akerman Senterfitt

"Aspatore's *Inside the Minds* series allows strategic professionals to access cutting-edge information from proven experts in the field. Their approach of providing consolidated, valuable, current information reflects their true understanding of the life of an executive. We need the best information in the most concise format. Aspatore is a consistently reliable resource that provides great information without expending unnecessary time." – Kimberly L. Giangrande, Principal, Intuitive HR

"A terrific compilation of real world, successful strategies and practical advice." – Sig Anderman, CEO, Ellie Mae Inc.

"Must read source for leaders wanting to stay ahead of emerging best practices and to understand the thought processes leading up to the innovation." – Mark Gasta, SVP and Chief Human Resources Officer, Vail Resorts Management Company

"A refreshing collection of strategic insights, not dreary commonplaces, from some of the best of the profession." – Roger J. Magnuson, Partner, Dorsey & Whitney LLP

"Unique and insightful perspectives. Great to read and an excellent way to stay in touch. – Filippo Passerini, President of Global Business Services and CIO, The Procter & Gamble Company

"A must read for C-level and senior executives. The information is based on actual experiences from successful senior leaders and has real, practical value presented in a very useable format." – Stephen Fugale, VP and CIO, Villanova University

"Some of the best insight around from sources in the know" – Donald R. Kirk, Shareholder, Fowler White Boggs PA

"Powerful insight from people who practice every day!" – Andrea R. Bortner, VP, GCSD Human Resources, Harris Corporation

"Aspatore's *Inside the Minds* series provides practical, cutting edge advice from those with insight into the real world challenges that confront businesses in the global economy." – Michael Bednarek, Partner, Shearman & Sterling LLP

"Outstanding insights from respected business leaders." – R. Scot Sellers, CEO, Archstone

ASPATORE

www.Aspatore.com

Aspatore Books, a Thomson Reuters business, exclusively publishes C-Level executives (CEO, CFO, CTO, CMO, Partner) from the world's most respected companies and law firms. C-Level Business Intelligence™, as conceptualized and developed by Aspatore Books, provides professionals of all levels with proven business intelligence from industry insiders—direct and unfiltered insight from those who know it best—as opposed to third-party accounts offered by unknown authors and analysts. Aspatore Books is committed to publishing an innovative line of business and legal books, those which lay forth principles and offer insights that when employed, can have a direct financial impact on the reader's business objectives. In essence, Aspatore publishes critical tools for all business professionals.

Inside the Minds

The *Inside the Minds* series provides readers of all levels with proven legal and business intelligence from C-Level executives and lawyers (CEO, CFO, CTO, CMO, Partner) from the world's most respected companies and law firms. Each chapter is comparable to a white paper or essay and is a future-oriented look at where an industry, profession, or topic is heading and the most important issues for future success. Each author has been selected based upon their experience and C-Level standing within the professional community. *Inside the Minds* was conceived in order to give readers actual insights into the leading minds of top lawyers and business executives worldwide, presenting an unprecedented look at various industries and professions.

Talent Management Strategies

Leading HR Executives on Bridging Generation Gaps, Facilitating Knowledge Transfer, and Creating an Effective Succession Plan

ASPATORE

Inside the Minds Project Manager, Erica Hartnett; edited by Jo Alice Darden; proofread by Melanie Zimmerman

Aspatore books may be purchased for educational, business, or sales promotional use. For information, please e-mail West.customer.service@thomson.com.

ISBN 978-0-314-27207-2

For corrections, updates, comments or any other inquiries please e-mail TLR.AspatoreEditorial@thomson.com.

First Printing, 2010
10 9 8 7 6 5 4 3 2 1

Mat# 41097072

CONTENTS

Engaging a Workforce That Will Grow the Company

Marie Mann

Vice President, Human Resources

Neopost USA Inc.

ASPATORE

Introduction

Neopost USA is a company going through significant transformation and change. Just three short years ago, it was six distinct organizations with different leadership, objectives, and ways of working. The last two years have been completely focused on combining those companies into one, even as we completed additional acquisitions.

Neopost USA is the U.S. subsidiary of a French-owned publicly traded parent, Neopost SA, which provides mailroom and shipping solutions across the world through both direct and dealer channels. Neopost is the second-largest company in its category worldwide and the largest in Europe. Neopost USA has more than 1,500 employees in the United States, including our direct employees and twelve company-owned dealers. Our locations include twenty-one branch sales offices in most major U.S. cities, our call center in Dallas, Texas, distribution center in Memphis, Tennessee, and corporate headquarters in Milford, Connecticut.

As the HR leader in the United States, reporting to the chief executive officer (CEO), and as a member of the executive team, I have the accountability for integrating and aligning our talent management strategy with our business objectives and building programs and practices that support our new employee-driven value proposition as we continue to reinforce our unified, one-company strategy.

Successful Talent Management

Talent management is ultimately all about your desire to retain the best and the brightest. So when we talk about talent management, we talk about the full lifecycle of our employees, which has several different components:

Component 1: Attract and Recruit the Best

It all starts with how you attract and recruit new talent into your company. Even in a difficult, tight economy, a growth-oriented company intending to outlast its competitors over the long haul will take a long-term perspective and ensure that good messages and strong employment branding in the market will continue to attract the right kind of people. If a company doesn't get this foundational step right, the rest of its talent strategy doesn't matter. Nothing is more important that hiring the right people; they are your company's future.

Our company has created and developed a compelling employment brand that has become our foundation for the rest of our whole people strategy. Unless you have worked for a competitor, typically people don't know much about Neopost USA, so we spend a great deal of time building a culture that we can describe to candidates as part of our discussion about why this is a great place to work. When a company already has that brand recognition, perhaps it is a bit easier to stimulate a potential recruit's interest in your company. We, however, have to do more work developing a compelling value proposition for why someone would want to work here versus a company with that well-known brand name. There are probably many companies like us out there that are smaller to mid-sized and not as well known, but they are nevertheless interesting and engaging places to work if the right foundation has been set. At Neopost USA, we believe the value chain is employees first, customers second, and shareholders third. This is based on the premise that if we treat our employees well, they, in turn will take good care of our customers, which will lead to stronger business results.

Once we have identified the people in whom we are most interested, our next step is to recruit them. We need to make sure our recruiting efforts are balanced between evaluating candidates and selling them on our opportunities. We begin with the evaluation, learning who the candidates are, what they know, their skills and abilities, and how these match the positions for which we are interviewing—in other words, what they "*can* do". Then we look at their desire and motivation to do our kind of work in our kind of company—what they "*will* do." Finally, we look at cultural fit. Every company has its own unique culture, and some people will simply fit better into a culture like ours that it is not overly corporate or structured than into the kind they might experience in a larger company.

After we find people who have the attributes we are looking for, we talk about our value proposition. Once we have evaluated that they can do the job, will do the job, and are a good fit for the company, then the balance in power shifts, and we start selling them on why this is a good place for them, based on the things they told us are important to them. We try to match our values with what we have learned about theirs through the interview process. As HR professionals and professional hiring managers, we all know that when a candidate derails, it is rarely because of lack of skill, but rather a mismatch in cultural fit and workplace behavior.

Component 2: On-Boarding and Orienting

The first part of our talent management strategy is about attracting and recruiting. The second part happens once they accept our offer. Then the focus shifts to on-boarding and orienting our new talent into the company. We want to make sure we get our new people off to a good start. This is a great example of where the human resources team has a shared responsibility and partnership with our line managers.

Our HR team works closely with our hiring managers to put together a checklist containing tasks they need to do their first day, their first week, their first month, and so on, to make sure our new hire experiences a smooth on-boarding process. We periodically host a formal new-hire orientation program where we bring in many of our senior executives to talk about our company, their roles, and the functions they lead. We introduce our new hires to some of the tools they may need as part of their lifecycle with us; we introduce them to our online learn center and to the self-service features of our human resource information system. At this stage, we want to reinforce our message that these employees have joined a great company.

Component 3: Training and Development

The third piece to managing talent concerns training and development. We believe good training is a combination of not only the experience employees receive on the job, but also the trainings that the manager or mentor exposes them to, as well as online training and tools. We offer instructor-led trainings given by different training departments determined by where you work. If you join our technical staff, as an example, we provide substantial technical training as new products are developed. We also have a sales-education team that works with our sales staff to reinforce the value of consultative selling and takes them through a series of courses, both online and instructor-led,

10

that help them learn about our product lines and the office solutions we sell. Our managers participate in a management development curriculum that includes content to help them maximize their effectiveness in managing others. Some module examples include goal-setting, performance management, progressive discipline, and delivering feedback, to name a few.

Beyond these specific types of training, we also have more generic training for every employee. This training focuses on reinforcing our employment brand, our company's value proposition, and the behavioral expectations we have for our employees.

Because we are a company that is composed of several merged entities, we didn't have one unified culture—each area of the business had its own unique culture. As a result, we introduce new people to our single, new culture. We help them understand our company's value proposition, which was created by our employees. Our value proposition communicates to every employee why the company exists and how each of us as individuals can create a great customer experience. Consequently, much of our training has been focused on reinforcing six key desired behaviors we believe are important to fulfill our company's value proposition. We have developed training in these key behaviors, so that everyone will understand what each means. They are accountability, adaptability, communicative, customer centricity, team-oriented, and knowledgeable.

Another focus for our training is performance management, an important part of talent development. While we do have a formal annual performance review process that we expect everyone to go through, we also encourage managers to at least hold quarterly discussions with their employees about their careers so that performance management does not center on just one annual event. Instead, it happens all the time in ongoing dialogues between managers and employees. The formal process is done online, and people are evaluated based on two criteria. One is how they measure against goals they created the prior year, and the other is how they measure against those six key behaviors mentioned above. We weave these six key behaviors into our entire talent management strategy so receiving feedback on the behaviors is critical to one's development in our company.

There are three parts to the annual performance management process:

1. Self-assessment: The employee builds a self-assessment of his or her skills and abilities as they relate to these behaviors and how they reached their goals.

2. Manager assessment: The manager also completes an online assessment of the employee's performance evaluating the same criteria.

3. In-person performance review meeting: The two have the opportunity to discuss their perceptions of the individual's performance, where they agree, and if they don't, what they need to build together to close the gaps.

We have a five-point rating system where a score of "5" means a person consistently exceeds expectations in that particular area. For select positions, we have also introduced 360-degree feedback where the review contains not only the self-assessment and the management's assessment, but also assessments from peers and subordinates. In some cases, external clients or customers will also weigh in. I have found that on the occasions where we have used this, the review has been extremely useful in helping people capitalize on their strengths, understand how they are perceived by others versus how they see themselves, where their blind spots are (and what to do about them), and how to close any gaps. In this way, we help people identify their own development opportunities. Our long-term goal is to use 360-degree feedback throughout the whole company. We keep it simple, asking four basic open-ended questions and asking the raters to provide an assessment on the same five-point scale of our six key behaviors.

Component 4: Succession Planning

Another important component of our talent management strategy is succession planning. HR works closely with our senior team to develop a list of key employees and senior people whose development we want to focus on because they are in line to be our future leaders. We have used a tool called the "9 box," which was originally developed by GE when they evaluated performance and potential. We use it to help categorize people in terms of skills and behaviors. From the matrix, we can determine the balance of skills for their position, the potential to do other work, and, of course, our six key behaviors. This simple framework has thus helped us think about people and where they could fit over the longer term.

Component 5: Reward and Recognition

The last piece of our talent management strategy is work recognition, which is what we often refer to as "love and money." Let's talk about "love"—a strong word, but in the workplace it simply means that people want to feel valued; they want to feel that what they do matters, that they make a difference, that they have a "line of sight" between what they contribute and the company's objectives. They want to know that someone cares about them. We often tell managers, people just want to hear a simple "Thank you! You did a great job! We appreciate your contribution!" "Money," of course, is being paid properly and the perception that the company has fair compensation practices. Neopost USA offers comprehensive benefits and a generous bonus plan that is tied to the company's results, as well as an individual's personal contributions. Overall, our total compensation and reward structure is generous and reinforces our desired behaviors.

Aside from financial compensation, the other component of this strategy is giving psychological/emotional rewards for working in the company. Everyone wants to feel that what they do matters, and everybody wants to feel they make a difference. Realizing this, we want to create a culture of recognition, so in the last couple of years we developed a program called "Neo Stars" that builds on reinforcing our six key behaviors. This reward and recognition program has three levels, all of which are peer- or customer-nominated, and all are selected by an employee committee:

1. A Silver Star offers a small cash value and a "silver certificate" noting the behavior that was displayed.

2. The Gold Star is the core of the program. We acknowledge at least six or eight people per quarter with a Gold Star—a little trophy that is shaped like a star. The important thing about winning a Gold Star (besides also receiving a $500 cash award) is that it shows you are recognized by your peers as a valuable employee

who displays our six key behaviors. This reward is not something that the leadership team determines; rather, people are nominated by their peers, by customers, or maybe even by their bosses or somebody else's boss. The idea is that anyone can nominate anyone for a Gold Star because we truly want to highlight and acknowledge the people who display these behavioral attributes. These recipients are acknowledged publicly in our quarterly employee communication meetings, which are hosted by our executive leadership team members.

3. The Platinum Star goes to the one employee who the employee nominating committee believes is worthy, essentially, of being named "employee of the year." It comes with a beautiful Lucite "platinum" trophy and a $2,500 cash award.

If we get those five pieces right, attracting and recruiting, on-boarding, training and development, succession planning, and rewarding and recognizing, we will realize good end results—i.e., retention. Every company undergoes challenges with retention, even in tough times; after all, the best people will always pick up and leave if they don't like what is happening in their company or don't feel a connection to the company and its people. Today we are experiencing approximately 20 percent annualized turnover, which is about average. I believe much of our success has to do with the focus we have placed on employees and the programs we have developed during the past few years to encourage their development.

Other Strategies in Development: Career Pathing

Another component of training and development is career pathing. We are just at the tip of the iceberg with developing a career-path strategy for each of our individual functions. One challenge of our medium-size company is that we cannot promise someone we are recruiting that he or she will spend six months doing one thing, two years doing another, and then after that timeframe, they will receive a certain promotion. A person's career path is not always that prescribed because it depends on changing market conditions, their work performance, and where vacancies create new opportunities. Because these factors are not predictable, we can't always describe an exact career path.

To combat this challenge, we engaged a worldwide leading consulting company in talent management to create and help us communicate a career-banding and compensation structure. We have identified the criteria for each band so that all employees can understand how he or she "fits" into the structure and what skills are expected for each career band. This was another exercise to help us unify and align our multiple companies into one. Our mid-sized company has only eight career bands. For each band, we identified five key criteria and identified the skill requirements for each. The five criteria are: organization impact, people/project management, autonomy, customer influence, and knowledge/skills. We reviewed each individual position and determined how the skills required in the position mapped to a career band. The grids below illustrate the banding structure and the criteria for each level within the bands.

Career Band Structure

- The structure includes 9 bands from top to bottom (although only interns and temps will fall in the lowest band)
  - Sales employees are banded although a separate reward structure will be maintained.

Band 2	Senior Business Leadership
Band 3	Vice President/Sr Vice President
Band 4	Director/Sr Director
Band 5	Manager/Sr Manager
Band 6	Supervisor/Lead
Band 7	Individual Contributors - exempt
Band 8	Individual Contributors - non exempt - technical
Band 9	Individual Contributors - non-exempt - administrative and clerical
Band 10	Interns and temps

Sales Structure

Band	Title	Sales Role
Band 3	Vice President/Sr Vice President	VP Direct Sales
Band 4	Director/Sr Director	Regional Sales Director
Band 5	Manager/Sr Manager	Branch Manager
Band 6	Supervisor/Lead	Sales Manager, Area Manager
Band 7	Individual Contributors - exempt	Sr. Territory Manager, Territory Manager, Sr. Account Executive, Account Executive, Sales Representative

As we refine this further, we will start to develop career paths for each individual function. We do have a prescribed career path in our sales organization right now because they are the drivers in our company (see chart below). Although you often can't say with absolute certainty that someone will be in the job for only six months or two years, we can make slightly more accurate trajectories in sales because once employees reach certain measurable levels of sales performance, they become senior account executives, then territory managers and so on. On the other hand, employees who are working in a call center may have to wait for a supervisory position to open before they can be promoted.

	Definition of Criteria	Band 2 Senior Business Leadership	Band 3 Vice President	Band 4 Director
Organizational Impact	Level or nature of organizational accountability, e.g., Corporate, individual contributor and scope of influence e.g., visionary, execution, degree of innovation/problem-solving impact and judgment required to perform the job	Global or Corporate (e.g., country or multiple country) accountability. Leads strategic direction of operating companies or global function. Sets business growth and profitability objectives globally. Responsible for overall profitability. Critical role that has make or break consequences on the company. Requires solution of issues that may have unprecedented occurrences in global environment. (Visionary)	Corporate functional accountability. Leads strategic direction of functional area in support of company's vision. Responsible for function results. Sets functional goals and objectives. Formulates business plans and solutions across multiple dimensions (e.g., technical/functional, financial, staffing) (Strategic)	Leads a sub-function, multiple departments, or segment within a function. Leads facilitates and contributes directly in the development and achievement of functional strategy and objectives. Sets and executes functional goals and objectives. Brings together multiple concepts across departments to develop and turn vision into concrete financial/business results (Tactical/Strategic)
People/Project Mgmt	People management, nature/size/level of supervisory responsibilities, Project management, project or other non-people management skills required of the position	Determines global or corporate organizational structure. Leadership responsibility for operating company to deliver business results. Leads senior functional executives. Has overall P&L responsibility for area of responsibility.	Determines functional structure. Leadership responsibility for function to deliver business results. Manages senior level managers and directors. Has P&L or budget responsibility for function.	Determines department structure. Leadership responsibility for creating large department, multiple departments, or smaller function to deliver business results. Manages managers and high-level individual contributors. Manages budgets.
Job Autonomy	Degree of autonomy and types of decisions required of the role and level of direction received	Operates with a high level of freedom to make decisions and exercises broad discretion. Self-directing. Determines company objectives within global/corporate strategy. Provides global/corporate leadership to company.	Determines functional objectives within corporate strategy. Exercises broad discretion within functional area. Provides functional leadership to operating companies	Determines department objectives within corporate strategy. Exercises discretion within functional area. Self-managing.
Customer Influence	Level and complexity of external and internal customer relationships	Actively develops and manages complex relationships with internal and external constituents (e.g., board of directors, auditors, customers, post office). Identifies external trends, products, and services that are likely to shape the needs of customers in the near future. Sets company approach on how to drive customer satisfaction. Adapts communication style to influence, information and negotiate both internally and externally.	Actively develops and manages complex relationships with internal and external constituents (e.g., Neopost worldwide and customers). Identifies external trends, products, and services that are likely to shape the needs of customers in the near future. Sets function approach on how to drive customer satisfaction. Adapts communication style to influence, information and negotiate both internally and externally.	Develops and manages relationships with internal and external constituents (e.g., corporate, operating company, and customers). May identify external trends, products, and services that are likely to shape the needs of customers in the immediate needs and long-term goals. Sets department approach on how to drive customer satisfaction. Adapts communication style to influence, information and negotiate both internally and externally.
Knowledge & Skills	Breadth and depth of knowledge, specific skills, job-related experience to effectively perform job, required education	Very broad/deep knowledge of industry Leadership experience in similar or related industry Multiple, diverse discipline knowledge. Ability to understand drive profitability. Ability to champion business opportunities.	Very broad/deep knowledge of industry or function Functional leadership experience. Understand other disciplines. Ability to understand and manage budgets and profitability. Understands how function contributes to company success.	Detailed understanding of best practices in a defined area of expertise. Viewed as functional expert both internally and externally. Familiarity with several other areas of expertise. Managerial experience. Ability to understand and manage budgets and profitability. Understands how function contributes to company success.

Trends That Could Impact Talent Management Strategy

We have to consider we work with four generations in the workplace. When you attract and develop people, you want to make sure you understand their specific individual needs. For example, if you ask a baby boomer and a "Gen Y" about their career expectations, you will quickly find they have vastly different ideas about work.

Therefore, a good talent management team strategy focuses on the individual. Although you have to have a framework that spells out what you are trying to do for everyone, your managers need to understand that their individual people might have different needs and desires. Some people may want to work a predictable eight-hour day because they value good work-life balance. Other people, however, want you to know they will work hard and long hours, but in return expect significant reward—perhaps more money, a promotion, or both. At the risk of oversimplifying this—as managers, it is critical that we treat people the way *they* want to be treated and listen to and understand what is important to them. This is the key to retaining talent. We have to be able to distinguish one employee's needs and desires from another employee's needs and desires. Not all employees are the same. A strong manager understands this, and adapts his or her managerial style to the employee's needs.

Impact of the Economic Downturn

Our company is unique: In 2009, when the economy was changing, our company was undergoing a huge transition. On the one hand, we were closing down two of our largest locations in California and moving many of those positions to the East Coast. While the people on the West Coast were bemoaning their job losses, on the East Coast we were hiring more than 300 people. This big transition required us to perform a big balancing act. We first told the people who were losing their jobs that, over the course of the next twelve months, we would be winding down operations. Then, three months before they were going to be specifically affected, we gave them their individual notices so they would have time to plan their personal transition out of the company. During this time of transition, we also had to keep them engaged because it was good for our business, *and* it was important to send a message that we were taking care of our people, even though they were leaving.

We conducted a great deal of training for these people on change management and offered them workshops on transitioning their careers, writing résumés, interviewing, and job search skills. In addition, we moved some of the West Coast employees to the East Coast to provide knowledge transfer and training for the new hires who were replacing their displaced West Coast colleagues. Because it was a tough economy, we found that it was relatively easy to find talent in the market. Many local companies, as well as our key competitors, had been downsizing. There were so many talented people in our local market that we had more qualified candidates than we had roles to fill. We found that people were applying for jobs that were paying less than they had previously earned. As they went through our recruiting process and saw firsthand the kind of company we were building, they were interested in working for us with or without pay comparable to their previous positions. I think it is fair to say the state of the economy had a significant positive impact on our ability to attract strong talent.

Our experience through this recession was different than many other companies. For example, through all of the challenge of the economy and a tough market, Neopost USA actually grew 2 percent in 2009. We are proud of our focus and ability to grow both top and bottom line in what many consider a shrinking market.

The other impact of the economy was better retention of talent. During this recession, we all read, heard about, or experienced firsthand, many companies cutting back on benefit levels, 401(k) plan matches, pay raises, and training. These reductions can have a big impact on your talent management strategy. We too, had challenges to reach our financial targets—and to grow sometimes means cutting back on special programs or training—which is why we chose to implement so many of these programs without the support of outside consultants. This do-it-yourself culture had the added benefit of development for our own HR colleagues.

For-profit business needs to be profitable. However, when you are not growing the top line, the only way you can maintain your profitability is to make cuts. Unfortunately, such tactics do affect talent. People desire to work for a company committed to their development; however, they define it, and when they see benefits and other training being cut back, their level of engagement can diminish.

Role of Work-Life Programs and Communications Practices

Underlying our five-bucket talent management strategy are characteristics such as our culture, communication style, and programs that support the strategy. Among these offerings are our work-life programs. Many of our employees in our key locations (corporate HQ, call center, and distribution center) are locally based and desire work-life balance. Some employees work either a part-time schedule or one with flexible work hours because they want to accommodate their personal circumstances. They might work 7 to 3 or 9 to 5, or even 10 to 7. Offering flextime has been quite helpful and proves over and over again to be a psychological benefit.

Another factor that supports our successful talent management strategy is our practice of engaging in two-way communication. We are committed to having open communications with our employees, which we do in a number of different ways. Having dialogue with and receiving feedback from employees helps strengthen the talent management strategy because people want to stay with companies where they see the leaders as open and receptive to their ideas. Employees appreciate the opportunity to speak freely about their perceptions of the company and offer suggestions to improve and progress.

As an example, we conduct a quarterly town-hall meeting for employees featuring presenters who are members of the leadership team or people who are involved in a special project or key initiative. In the interest of keeping the communication open, we always cover our financial status, as well as our reward and recognition program. We also present a snapshot of our progress with projects so that everyone in the company knows where we stand relative to achieving our corporate key initiatives and how their roles fit in. If they can perceive the connection between their everyday jobs and what the company is trying to accomplish, they will feel much more engaged and, consequently, likely to remain with the company.

We also publish an e-newsletter every other month and periodic updates. In calendar year 2010, our e-newsletter has become *the* go-to place for company updates and information. Because of the electronic format, it is easy to disseminate and puts the onus on the employee to find the articles that are of greatest interest to them. In addition, in 2010, we sent out more than 300 different electronic communications and announcements in an effort to keep everyone informed of changes in the business, key wins in the marketplace, and news items about new employees or employee changes or promotions. We have found these two tools extraordinarily helpful in unifying our employee base. We also realize that with a geographically dispersed employee base, not everyone has access to leadership all the time, so whenever possible we conduct small group meetings with our leadership so that people have access to the leaders in an open forum where they can ask questions and have dialogue with our leaders.

Advice to HR Executives for Managing Talent

HR executives who manage talent should have a plan, communicate it, and help people understand how their roles fit into the bigger picture.

Also, remember that everyone is tightly focused on himself or herself. Consequently, even though you are trying to execute an overriding strategy, you should also convey to people that someone is paying attention to their individual needs; someone cares about them; and someone thinks that what they do matters. The more you can personalize that message and the better you can train your managers to have those kinds of conversations, the more successful you will be. Unfortunately, HR cannot do this alone. When it comes to people, every success is a shared experience between HR and the leaders, managers, and employees. We are all here to improve, to progress, to get better each and every day. My overarching advice is to be inclusive, collaborative, and involved in the transformation of the company to make it better by involving your people.

Key Takeaways

- By definition, talent management encompasses an employee's full work-life cycle.

- Talent management is ultimately all about your desire and ability to retain the best and the brightest.

- Recruiting efforts should be balanced between evaluating candidates and selling them on the company's opportunities, as those relate to their interests.

- A good talent management team strategy focuses on the individual. Even though you are trying to execute an overriding strategy, you should also convey to people that someone is paying attention to their needs, interests, and career aspirations; someone cares about them; and someone thinks that what they do matters.

- If employees can perceive the connection between their everyday jobs and what the company is trying to accomplish, they will be more engaged and, consequently, likely to remain with the company.

- Advice to HR executives in managing talent: Have a plan linked to the corporate objectives and initiatives; communicate it; and help your employees understand how their role and contributions fit in.

Marie Mann is an award-winning HR executive who was named "HR Leader of the Year" in 2009 by the Southern Connecticut Chapter of the Society of Human Resources Management. She currently serves as vice president of human resources (HR) for Neopost USA, an international mailing and shipping solutions company, headquartered in France. In her current role, she is charged with leading the cultural transformation, integration, and value proposition positioning of Neopost USA to help the company attain its goal of becoming the fastest-growing mailing solutions company in the United States. Ms. Mann is a member of Neopost USA's twelve-person Executive Leadership Team and reports directly to the chief executive officer for North America.

Ms. Mann's broad experience includes leading HR strategy in fast-paced organizations experiencing transformation and change. She has worked both internally in executive HR roles and externally as a consultant in diverse industries in both creative and traditional businesses, mid-sized newly merged companies, and large multi-national corporations.

Prior to joining Neopost USA, Ms. Mann was senior vice president of HR for Remy Cointreau USA, a luxury brand spirits company, where she led multiple change initiatives linking HR to the company's business strategy. Prior to Remy, Ms. Mann was chief people officer at AKQA, a global new media company; executive vice president of human resources at AGENCY.COM and global advertising agency, Saatchi & Saatchi; and vice president of human resources for the professional publishing division of Times Mirror Corporation. Prior to those positions, she spent her career in talent management roles in large, global professional services firms.

Ms. Mann has her MS and EdS in counseling psychology from the State University of New York at Albany, and her BS from Wagner College. In addition, since joining Neopost, USA, she has completed two executive development programs at L'Ecole des Hautes Etudes Commerciales *in France.*

Dedication: *This chapter is dedicated to my current employer, Neopost USA, and my past employers who have all helped me develop my philosophies and ideals about strong HR business partnership and managing talent.*

Closing the Generation Gap and Growing Your Talent

James A. Sennish

Vice President, Human Resources

Firelands Regional Medical Center

ASPATORE

Introduction

I am the vice president of human resources for Firelands Regional Medical Center in Sandusky, Ohio. We are located on the southern shore of Lake Erie, midway between Cleveland and Toledo. As a regional medical center providing advanced care and services, Firelands Regional Medical Center serves a significant market share from the counties of Erie, Ottawa, Sandusky, and Huron, resulting in a regional services area of more than 300,000 residents.

Firelands Regional Medical Center is locally managed and governed as a not-for-profit health care facility. Our economic impact in the local communities in 2009: 1,943 employees; 234 medical staff members representing more than thirty-five specialties; 10,815 inpatients; 26,692 visits for outpatient services; 48,130 emergency room visits; and 681 births.

My role in the organization consists of all the traditional human resource responsibilities—employee benefits, compensation, recruitment, training, and development. I am also a part of the senior management team, and I try to incorporate human resource considerations into the major decisions of the hospital as a whole. Firelands Regional Medical Center is an economic engine for the community and a safety net for those in need. It is a lean organization, and we are holding our own in these difficult times.

Farming Our Own Talent

One part of our company's talent management strategy is to ask every member of our senior management team to have a succession plan for each of their key positions. Because we serve a primarily rural population and are not the most diverse county, we know that growing and retaining our own employees is a key strategy. To further educate our staff, we have a tuition reimbursement program for nursing and allied health that pays 100 percent tuition reimbursement.

Like many hospitals, in becoming the lean organization we have needed to be, we were not left with many assistant directors, assistant vice presidents, or assistant managers. As such, we realized early that there is not a good farming system readily available to us and we would consequently need to develop our own managers. We like to identify the up-and-comers—the employees who want to do more for the organization—and try to point them into careers or academics where they will be able to get the skills they need to move up, and then give them different opportunities here.

Even though an employee might not hold a certain position, we try to give our employees opportunities to be members of teams that undertake new projects or new endeavors. Most of the senior management team knows that an official mentoring relationship or just being available to help is a key part of growing and retaining our employees. The bottom line is we understand that we have a greater opportunity to grow our own than to attract this kind of talent in the general market and throughout the state, region, or even the country.

Workforce Demographics

Our organization largely consists of the baby boomer generation; in fact, I think just about everybody on our senior management team is a member, and keeping up with the reading and understanding that we are reflective of the country as a whole has influenced how our talent management practices have evolved. This is coupled with the fact that 83 percent of our employees are female, and, not surprisingly in these difficult economic times, they are the primary providers of health care benefits for their spouses and families. So the combination of these two factors is an important consideration in our decision-making as we pursue our goals of high patient and employee satisfaction.

We understand that being a family-friendly workplace with good pay and benefits goes a long way toward keeping us the employer of choice. As a result, we thankfully do not have a high turnover rate as an organization or in management positions, as we feel we are providing for the needs of our employees on many levels, as reflected in our *Modern Healthcare* magazine's Best Places to Work in Healthcare ranking of #38 in its list of Top 100 Healthcare Organizations.

When we do have to go out to recruit for top-level positions, we utilize headhunters, but often there are few candidates from whom to select. While we love where we live—we are right on Lake Erie and the Lake Erie Islands vacation land—it is difficult to find someone from a large metropolitan area with the skills we need who is looking for the kind of life and environment we offer in our location.

Providing In-House Incentives

Since we understand that situation, we make an equal or maybe even greater effort to help our own employees grow and provide them with additional benefits and incentives to stay on board. For example, we established a scholarship fund for the children of employees who are going into medical fields. Through this fund, we are able to provide seventeen to twenty annual scholarships in amounts of $1,000 or $2,000 each. As we are able to do this each year, we have gained some loyalty from both our employees and their children. When they do internships, we are right there and willing to help them. While we recognize that this is not the only way to achieve loyalty, we have found that it does help.

Additionally, if we have a high-ranking position open that we anticipate will be difficult to fill, we offer a $5,000 employee referral bonus. We can truly see the six degrees of separation theory in play—it is amazing when a dietary person has a cousin who has a friend who would be a perfect fit for the open position. We love to give the bonus out that way, and we make a big deal of it whenever we can to make the referring employee feel they have won the prize. It creates chatter, and it gets to be fun after a while knowing there are employees with family and friends all over the country who can be the right fit for us. People get excited when we send out an all-user e-mail that mentions the employee referral bonus. People enjoy that feeling and the reward, so we celebrate the referral in our newsletter. It is another one of those little efforts that we hope will pay off in the long run. Again, it is not a complete solution, but it is another piece of the puzzle with which we have been happy.

Talent Management Trends

I think the number one trend an HR executive should be aware of when formulating and revising talent management policies and procedures is that much of the talent is attracted to big cities, so you cannot expect or assume that any outside talent will relocate to a small rural town. Second, it is important to establish good relationships with any young up-and-comers within the organization, share whatever information you can with them, be open to them, and encourage them to take advantage of learning opportunities.

Another consideration is that senior management teams are currently largely made up of the baby boomer generation. The average age on our senior management team is fifty-something, so we are trying to come up with a plan on how to share knowledge, not just through textbooks and magazines, but also by sharing what one has learned throughout one's career. We need to make sure when the day comes and someone wants to retire that a knowledge shift or sharing can take place. It is probably a good idea for each of us to have journals that we can provide for the transition and be aware that they are of value and interest.

We need to think about how we can refine the journals to help with those inevitable transitions that will occur. Hopefully, there will be the opportunity for a planned knowledge transfer instead of just finding out a transition is needed when someone walks in with two weeks' notice. It will be important to consider how we can continue grooming our own because our trend over the last five years has been to fill positions in upper management with local talent, as opposed to drawing talent from a larger area.

Mentoring Strategies

We do not have a formal mentoring program in place as part of our talent management strategy, but we do mentoring. When there is a new director somewhere in the organization, I will go out of my way to help however I can, and in several of those promotions I have offered to be a mentor, and several of my colleagues have done this, as well. It is not as formal a program as I would like it to be, but we look for areas the person can use some help in, and then one of us will take on that mentoring role.

The part of our program that I like is that periodically we do training for the leadership team on mentoring and begin the session by asking the audience who was a mentor for them and to share their experiences. The answers never cease to amaze me and usually take the form of the mentor establishing a meaningful human connection and genuinely caring for and listening to the mentee.

We try to make the mentoring experience a give-and-take scenario, rather than telling them to just listen and let us show them the way. As a matter of fact, we remind mentors that "The good Lord gave you two ears and one mouth. He probably meant for you to listen twice as much as you talk." Mentoring is similar because you want to hear from the mentees and understand what they are thinking. For instance, a newly promoted director of one of our allied health departments was full of excitement to tackle her responsibilities, but she discovered that the staff was subtly resistant to changes she was trying to implement and questioning her authority. She was focused on these issues, and if I hadn't been listening to what she was experiencing, I would have used our time together concentrating on how labor and productivity should be managed, rather than how to deal with these employee relations issues that were actually where she needed help.

Part of the mentoring process is that we are not just trying to train someone to do a job and not get the wrong idea of what it is, but also listening to them, helping them find the answers if we do not have them, and showing them how we work collaboratively, since none of us knows everything. When we've talked to mentees about their experience, they usually say that the best part was that the mentor was like a friend they could share workplace frustrations with, that the mentor listened and offered ideas instead of simply telling them what they were supposed to do.

Taking a Risk on Young Blood

I think as a senior management team, we are quite cohesive and work together to develop our talent management strategy because we all understand that as a workforce we are getting older. We recently had the opportunity to fill a vice president of operations position, obviously a key role in our organization. We had a thirty-year-old gentleman who was an assistant vice president, and over the last five years each of us in senior management had worked with him to prepare for a future opportunity such as this. Even though this open position was a huge responsibility for a thirty-year-old, we gave him the opportunity. He has tremendous support within the leadership team, particularly from our chief executive officer

(CEO), who has given him many learning opportunities and involved him in meetings and discussions not typically available to this position.

Our new vice president of operations, the vice president of nursing, and the senior vice president and chief nursing officer are working together more as a team now. There is great enthusiasm from this well-educated young man we promoted, and he has had a good foundation here to prepare himself for this new position, along with a great deal of continued support to make sure he succeeds. I have been in the workforce for thirty-one years, and I know that if people want you to succeed, most times you will. This gentleman is stepping up to the challenges—putting in many hours, coming in on weekends, etc. In return, I believe the organization has gained a measure of loyalty by giving him a career opportunity that's hard to duplicate. He is loyal, grateful, and eager to do what he can to help the organization succeed. There is so much positive energy in that. Every once in a while, I will bring him into my office, and we will talk about a certain decision he has to make. There is a beauty to making decisions on the fly, but I also try to share my experiences with him, along with ideas and considerations to help him make difficult decisions when the options are not always black-and-white in their presentation.

I do not know what kind of vice president of operations we could have gotten from somewhere else, but I do know we got a young, well-trained, enthusiastic person whose success we all have a stake in. This is one example of how our senior management in all departments has come together to help implement our talent management development strategy.

Bridging the Generation Gap

Throughout history, elders gave the wisdom to the young people, and even though we have a bit of an older population in our organization, I think what has helped us bridge the gap in generations is our move to an electronic medical record process.

It occurred to us early that there was a skill shift. We realized that the younger generation might not know as much about nursing, but they know a great deal about computers and technology, and they have a comfort level with it that many of the older generation do not have. Even for me, while I try to stay current, it is amazing how many times I have to call my college-aged kids to ask them how to do something or ask them what something is.

The main challenge with the younger generation is that they need to slow down. I do not learn as rapidly as they do. When we realized we were going to have a totally electronic medical record in five years, and we started this about two years ago, everybody knew there was no option to go back to paper if they did not like it. As a result, when everyone knew the paper method would disappear, there was a transformation in how our older workers viewed our younger workers. The younger workers are now sought out and appreciated, and sometimes the older workers literally bake them cookies. Even with things like doing their self-evaluation on a paperless system, an older worker will pull a younger person close by for help.

Now, when we bring younger employees into the organization, a part of the interview and their orientation is letting them know how they can help the older generation become more literate in the language of computer technology in a paperless world. That is what I have found remarkable in my career—young people are so fresh and excited when they enter the workforce, and if you can just slow them down a bit, they could truly serve as a great balance to the older employees. Periodically, I will call a young staff member into my office to ask for help, and I am sure they feel good about it. Not to overplay it, but I think the fact that the older generation has been seeking out the younger generation for help has been huge for us in closing the generation gap.

The Changing Workforce

There will certainly be changes in the workforce, so talent or knowledge sharing will become critical. Ideally, I think we all need to get into the habit of putting down our thoughts on paper or in the computer journal. Of course, while I know there are times when that would not be appropriate, realistically, much of what I know is generally shared through a story or something someone says that sparks a discussion.

We are trying to be more disciplined about our knowledge transfer, so when a terrific idea comes up, we need to make an effort to write it down so that we have a record of the who, what, where, when, how, and why of it. Even if you just start jotting down a few quick notes, you can later flesh it out with formal paragraphs and more organization to your thoughts and ideas. Eventually, if you are in a mentoring situation, there could be a combination of methods used—instead of just sharing advice from memory, you can pull out your journal and share those things you may have thought of over the years that may now help someone else. What is more interesting than the story of you? Knowledge is not meant to be hoarded. It is meant to be shared liberally. This is the mantra of what we are trying to do: write your ideas down and share that knowledge.

You might be surprised to find that what you thought was the most important thing in your job five years ago may not be the same as it is today. That is some proof that you are never finished learning or adjusting, but there are also nuggets of information in your notes on how you dealt with difficult situations that are timeless. We are trying to foster a culture of sharing and helping, and this should be something each of us *wants* to do instead of something we *have* to do. We call it our ACE philosophy: Attitude, Commitment, and Enthusiasm. We take these areas into account when we conduct evaluations and performance appraisals. When someone is hired, we look at his or her ACE. We have developed questions that help find out whether the candidate possesses these traits, and we use this to help make hiring and promotion decisions. We also incorporate ACE into our orientation and training programs, as we feel it lends itself to our patient and employee satisfaction efforts.

After a number of years, it is our hope that these traits will become a natural way of doing business. By establishing an ACE culture that is based on learning, sharing, and believing in each other, we believe the staff will be fully engaged in the hospital's mission and the institution's continued success.

Keys to Success

If I were to provide advice to up-and-coming HR executives, I would tell them to be as open-minded and creative as they can be with whatever aspects of the job they can. As HR executives, we have to make sure we take time to talk to people, get them excited, and help them grow in their knowledge and skills, and we need everybody's experience to meet future workplace challenges. As difficult as the future may be, we cannot let any artificial or racial barriers become factors. It goes back to that fundamental thing—we are mainly attracting our talent regionally, so it is important to be aware that you may have to grow your own talent, and the best time to start that is right now. I do not think there is any hard formula for success, but the more open and creative you can be, the more successful you will be.

Technology Trends

We have been using a paperless performance management system for several years that serves as the basis of our talent management system. At the core of this system is an annual review of every employee's job description that is part of the employee completing his or her self-evaluation, including proposed goals and objectives for the coming year. Often, these goals and objectives include coursework, seminars, and/or preparation for additional certifications. These self-evaluations are then reviewed by the employee's director and edited, and then the two have the performance interview.

This performance interview includes not only a discussion of the employee's recent job performance, but also a discussion of future goals and career development. This is the opportunity for the leader and the employee to have a meaningful discussion about the employee's career path and what opportunities may be available in the future. The system allows for both the leader and the employee to keep a journal creating an efficient way to log these discussions. These journals are also an effective way for employees and managers to document other personal and professional accomplishments that not only are of value for the performance appraisal process, but also help them down the road when they are interviewed for possible promotions within the organization.

Our third-party provider for our paperless performance appraisal system also offers a quality talent management package that will more than likely be our next technology step as we formalize our talent management efforts. As part of our 2010 goals and objectives, our CEO has asked each member of the senior management team to have a viable succession planning document for his or her areas of responsibility. As we develop these succession planning documents, we are using the paperless performance appraisal system as the basis and plan to have a seamless transition of information when we add the talent management platform to our existing system.

A third aspect of our technology efforts is our eLearning system that is our Internet-based education management system. The purposes of the program are to help us develop and deliver a wide range of training and education for all of our employees and to have the ability to track and manage these training records. Through this system, we are able to track mandatory education, continuing education, hospital-specific courses, Webinars, competencies, and ongoing nursing education. Most of the course offerings are self-paced, interactive, and available at any time on a computer with Internet access capability. When you consider the busy lives and schedules of our employees, our eLearning system allows our employees to keep their skills up-to-date in a convenient format that doesn't require travel and time away from their families. The overall benefits to the hospital from the eLearning system are many, including the enhancement of our ability to deliver timely and relevant education to our employees in an efficient and cost-effective manner.

To summarize, our use of technology in the areas of our paperless performance appraisal system, combined with our succession planning efforts and supported by our eLearning system, puts us in the best position to meet the future challenges of an ever-changing health care landscape.

Budgeting and Talent Management

I am not sure I will get a big budget for a formal talent management system anytime soon, but that doesn't mean we won't continue working on it. We work with our third-party administrators and health care advisers on many of our benefits, like pensions and investment options, and we have had conversations with them on how we can develop these to enhance our employee retention and talent management efforts. When the time is right, we will pursue a complete talent management program, and in the mean time, we will continue to recognize and reward our employees whenever possible. We believe our employee satisfaction efforts have produced a professional environment in which our employees still find time to have fun. Even in these difficult times, we still see the value of employee picnics and other family-based activities to complete the whole positive employment experience that lends itself to employee retention and talent management. This and our generous tuition reimbursement plan are probably our best tools right now for helping our employees' progress in their careers.

Company Success

The one thing I want to make clear is that our HR department has a key role in our organization, and I'm a valued member of our senior management team. I think that makes all the difference. We know what challenges the nurses have; we know what challenges the outpatient department has; and we are able to help in many areas.

I think we are able to show our value, even in these difficult times when the possibility of outsourcing HR is real. Our mantra among ourselves is that if we are not getting better, we are getting worse because people out there will provide our services, and we have to make sure that leadership always sees the value of an internal HR function. That encapsulates much of our effort, along with just trying to have a culture of learning because we are never finished learning, and because of that I think HR will always have a role.

I also want to mention that our organization has received some recognition —we were ranked number 38 in *Modern Health Care's* Best Places to Work in Health Care in the United States. We have been recognized by the Ohio Chamber of Commerce Best Employer's Award as #7 Large Employer. In addition, we have been recognized by the American Heart Association as a "Fit Friendly Company" for the last three years, and we have been recognized locally as the Best Place to Work for the last four years by Funcoast.com's reader's poll.

For several years, we used the Great Place to Work Institute for our Employee Engagement Surveys. They invited us to speak at their national conference because we had made the biggest turnaround in employee satisfaction in the shortest amount of time of any company that had participated in their survey, and they do a great job, by the way. They pick Fortune's Top 100 Companies, and they thought enough of what we were doing here to invite us to speak to an audience that included employees from Google and some of the other best companies. It was a highlight of my career. I think for a small rural hospital, we are doing some really good things and have gotten some nice recognition on the national level.

Key Takeaways

- The baby boomer generation currently makes up a large percentage of today's senior management. Consequently, it is important to prepare for the necessity of a widespread knowledge transfer.
- It is important to recognize the talent within your business and find ways to educate and train those employees with potential to move up in the ranks.
- Knowledge is meant to be shared, not hoarded; accurately record as much information as possible regarding who, what, when, where, why, and how.
- Encourage employees to follow the ACE philosophy: Attitude, Commitment, and Enthusiasm.
- Technology is here to stay and requires that everyone continue learning throughout his or her career. The older generation can learn from the younger generation

James A. Sennish, vice president, human resources, joined Firelands Regional Medical Center in March 2006. Previously he was director of human resources for Erie County and served the city of Sandusky in a number of positions. His responsibilities at Firelands include the administration of human resources for the Medical Center. He directs all human resources activities, including recruitment, retention, education, benefits, compensation, employee relations, and the human resources information system (HRIS), as well as human resources regulatory and governmental compliance.

Mr. Sennish has undergraduate and graduate degrees from Bowling Green State University.

Dedication: *To Nancy, Lynn, and Connie for their support in this and many other endeavors.*

Exceptional Talent Management Starts at the Top

Kareen M. Muros, SPHR
Vice President, Human Resources
Ovations Food Services LP

ASPATORE

Introduction

As vice president of human resources (HR) for Ovations Food Services, an affiliate of Comcast-Spectacor, I'm responsible for ensuring that our 8,300-plus employees have a compliant, respectful, stimulating, and high-growth-potential workplace. Ovations manages the foodservice operations for public assembly facilities such as arenas, stadiums, casinos, racetracks, ballparks, and convention centers. Because our business is in the leisure and recreation segment of the hospitality industry, HR has the added responsibility of making sure the workplace is fun—after all, our sports and entertainment employees are "part of the show," and a vital part of the guest experience.

As the second fastest-growing contract foodservice company in the United States, we open new facilities every month across the United States and in Canada. We are also diligently working on laying the groundwork for European and Asian operations. Creating overarching HR policies, procedures, and practices that uniformly apply to a wide range of employee classifications and geographical locations is often challenging. But our biggest challenge is having enough qualified managers in place to handle the aggressive growth mode that we're in.

We needed to shift from a traditional, reactive recruiting style to one that's more fluid and proactive. Our focus is on creating and executing aggressive people-planning strategies in the both the short and the long term, and not just for one or two positions. Our broad employee base spans every classification, from executives and exempt managers to the part-time, seasonal hourly workers who make up the majority of our labor force. That means we have had to tailor our recruitment techniques, practices, and objectives accordingly to effectively home in on the perfect hire within each classification. A rigorous one-size-fits-all recruitment policy does not work for us.

From an HR standpoint, working in the world of sports and entertainment is an exciting adventure. Each facility is a microcosm of everything HR-related that can possibly occur, both positive and negative. Starting with the recruitment process, HR has innumerable opportunities to develop unique, highly effective ways to shape and improve the workplace. We are also in an industry that is fraught with regulatory compliance challenges, occasional employee volatility, and an escalating need for more and more manager training. Not everyone is suited for a fast-paced, high-energy, diverse workplace that requires long hours and an unflagging commitment to excellence. Finding and hiring those exceptional candidates requires a creative technical and interpersonal approach by the HR team, as well as an increasingly greater investment of time and in budget. Approximately 32 percent of my overall HR budget is currently to allocated to talent management and sourcing, and that percentage climbs each year.

Hiring Strong Leaders = Building a Strong Talent Base

The corporate HR department puts most of its "fire power" into sourcing and hiring top managers and executives. Deciding who the leaders of our company will be is one of the most important decisions any company will make—and decisions that will determine the success or failure of a company for years to come. Talent management has to start at the top; without strong leaders in key positions, nothing happens, and success achieved through rapid growth cannot be sustained.

We're in a business in which the award of a new contract is often based on the strength of the candidate presented as our top leader for that facility. The client is aware that every operational decision affecting its profitability and success flows through or comes from this position. If the client doesn't feel confident in the candidate we've put forth, its decision-makers do not feel confident in awarding a major contract to our company. It's that simple. Our business is all about having the right person in the right place at the right time. That means that we have to have an exceptional leadership pipeline that can be relied on to produce the right-fit manager at a moment's notice.

And our managers have to "stick." Our contracts with clients, whether they are sports teams, private ownership groups, or municipalities, almost always contain provisions for ensuring continuity and retention of top managers. And there are punitive financial consequences if we've made a mistake in choosing our top leaders. That doesn't even factor in the high cost of attrition to the company in financial expenditure, loss of productivity, morale issues, etc. It is critical that HR and the hiring managers get it right the first time.

Making a Personal Connection

Technology (more, better, bigger, faster) is important to my HR team's success: instantaneous resume submissions and rapid-fire responses are the norm; anything slower than real time is unacceptable. But using more and faster technology in attracting applicants is just the starting point; technology might increase the pool of active more-or-less-qualified candidates, but it will not cinch the deal. It is not technology that makes an HR department successful; it is HR's ability to make a valuable and enduring personal connection with the candidate that determines a successful recruitment strategy.

Many traditional HR (personnel-type) departments are simply tasked with sourcing candidates: posting openings online, posting positions internally, identifying qualified and interested internal candidates, plowing through job boards and reverse searches, retaining recruiters, etc. The "real job" of driving the selection process has traditionally fallen to hiring managers. Not so at Ovations. HR is responsible for taking a leadership role at the onset by, first, identifying exceptional candidates (making the first-cut decision, beyond just sifting and sorting resumes) and, then, initiating that critical first contact. Establishing a personal connection with the best applicants quickly, confidently, and knowledgably has been instrumental in getting the hiring process off to a good start.

The second critical component of a highly effective recruitment effort is the "realistic job preview" (RJP). Providing the candidate with a truthful and knowledgeable description of "the good, the bad and the ugly" of the position builds credibility and trust. An honest and realistic description of the job, location, challenges, and so on, provides meaningful information to the candidate. A good HR recruiter does not want to be viewed as "selling" the job, but as someone who is discerning and qualitative (although, yes, it is a marketing process). This reassures the candidate that HR understands our business and can speak to the points the candidate most interested in. More important is that HR provides answers to unspoken questions and concerns, which also helps build credibility.

The third prong of Ovations' recruitment strategy is to find creative ways to source passive candidates. This is especially important in the contract foodservice industry, where there are just a handful of major players competing for the equally small pool of high-level executives and managers. The "recycling" of managers rotating through each of the major companies, sometimes more than once, depending on contract awards, is commonplace because of the limited number of qualified candidates. We strive to break out of this mold and distinguish ourselves as a company with a higher quality of manager by growing our own brand of manager internally and seeking talent in creative ways and places (not just from our competitors).

Recent Changes

Our talent management practices changed significantly over the past five years. The first reason is one shared by every other employer: as the baby boom generation nears retirement, the younger generation is often not sufficient in numbers or experienced enough to fill the gap. In a small industry, that translates into fierce competition for the top employees, the employees who can have a successful track record of delivering high-quality results. The best way to overcome this challenge is to build strong internal management development programs to fast-track talent.

Another impetus for taking our talent management practices to a new level is the current legal climate, and this does not appear to get better or easier in the future. The hospitality industry has become increasingly more complex to manage with respect to regulatory compliance (especially wage and hour compliance). Our lagging economy has resulted in a spike in employee grievances, Equal Employment Opportunity Commission (EEOC) complaints, and litigation, and general employee work preparedness is at an unacceptable low.

These areas alone have made the people-management part of a manager's job as big as or bigger than the technical or operations part of the job. And that means we need managers who are not only good operators, but who are also knowledgeable about employment law, the legal side of the regulatory process, training and development, and so on. Solid business acumen is not icing on the cake anymore; it has become a top requirement in our standard selection criteria. And failing to hire managers who already bring this knowledge to the table exposes the company to potential costly situations. Sourcing the most qualified, knowledgeable candidates requires casting a wider net and more thorough vetting.

Changing Roles for HR Management

The same economic, regulatory, and business complexities that made it necessary to hire better educated and more qualified managers has also made it necessary to hire better educated, professionally certified (Professional in Human Resources, or PHR, and Senior Professional in Human Resources, or SPHR), and more knowledgeable HR managers. The role of HR management has shifted from an administrative and support function to now being an integral part of the overall company management and decision-making process. Now that we have that proverbial seat at the table, HR management is expected to take the lead in shaping employment decisions. HR's role as administrator has evolved into a strategic adviser to the top executives of the company.

Just as solid operations experience and knowledge used to be the primary skill set for line managers and department heads, familiarity with the general body of HR knowledge used to be the main skill set of HR practitioners in our industry. As with operations managers, those skills are now just a baseline or starting point. The new HR manager must also be a skilled adviser, creative thinker, proactive problem-resolver, creative and highly effective trainer, and developer and "grower" of employees—and be really, really smart. Communication skills must be exceptional, and the new HR manager must be courageous enough to weigh in honestly with managers who do not take regulatory compliance seriously or have not kept current with changing laws. A successful HR practitioner must also be a lifelong learner, with a passion for reading trade and professional journals, learning about new software, understanding changing laws and regulations, and being a generalist extraordinaire.

Know Your Industry

It's no longer sufficient for an HR executive to be an expert in HR matters. It is absolutely imperative that any HR executive know as much as he or she can about *all* aspects of the business he or she is in—and the more, the better. He or she cannot advise or suggest any course of action without knowing how the operation works, including its objectives and challenges. And knowing as much as we can about our business extends to that all-important personal connection with top candidates.

The only way we in HR can make valuable suggestions or provide meaningful and sought-after recommendations to the president and chief operations officer (COO) is to have a thorough working knowledge of our business. An effective HR executive must know as much about the objectives, planned growth, challenges, key initiatives, financial health, etc., of the business as any operations, marketing, or finance vice president (VP) or senior vice president (SVP) would—not almost as much, but as much. That high-level knowledge is imperative in today's business climate.

Technology and Training

There is no shortage of information out there. HR practitioners need to be lifelong learners, so it is crucial to read everything you can, attend every conference you can, talk to people, get engaged, and read trade journals. The Web is also a phenomenal resource. We are currently redesigning our Web site to attract younger candidates. A Web site needs more zip and excitement and more appeal; it needs to be more interactive and quick. We also use social networking media, such as Twitter or Facebook, to get the word about us out there.

E-learning is something that we are expanding by developing more e-learning strategies on our Web site, though it has not been highly successful in the past. Our managers usually do not have MBAs or a great deal of business acumen; for them to understand business or HR concepts, especially concerning business or employee relations, you have to have examples that are tied to our industry. Often a generic e-learning program does not address our industry with specific examples. Follow-up is easier and more thorough if a presenter is involved in training. However, e-learning is good when you have to take care of mandatory training, such as sexual harassment or discrimination training, and you need people to be in compliance. It does not take the place of true learning, where you have a presenter and a small interactive group. In those situations, you can share ideas and make sure they understand.

One of the best benchmarks to measure success is how many of your people have been promoted, to what level, and how successful they have been.

Our number one initiative in the next year is to use more technology and customize it so it connects with our applicants to reflect what *they* are looking for in a career and in a professional lifestyle. Effective recruitment is not only about putting the company's brand out there; it's also about truly understanding what the candidate is looking for. We must understand what our applicants want, as well as what traits people who are successful in this industry have, and integrate these into our search process. This initiative will also help us in our efforts to foster diversity in our management.

Effects of the Economy on HR Strategies

We have more than one hundred facilities in almost every state of the union. We have operations in areas that are economically depressed and economically sound. In our industry, it does not matter whether the economy takes a downturn or prospers—we will always find outstanding candidates because we know how to search for them and how to attract them.

A soft economy certainly makes it easier to attract a more qualified and more engaged part-time worker. Of our 8,300 employees, about 90 percent are part-time workers who mainly want to work part-time. In a good economy, you typically get the underemployed or terminally unemployed workers, especially in economically not-so-prosperous areas, which is usually where arenas and stadiums are located. In a bad economy, you will have many high-quality employed people who need to supplement their incomes for a variety of reasons and they want to do it in a fun environment—something that is different from what they do during the daytime. As for salaried staff, the economy does not make much of a difference because the field is so narrow.

Conclusion

A weak economy has benefited the sports and entertainment business through an influx of better educated, more qualified, non-traditional part-time employees. This has resulted in several positive changes to our workplace, as well as challenges. A more qualified employee is more likely to be more engaged in the job and displays a higher degree of ownership and pride in excellent performance. They are more likely to make creative suggestions for process or service improvement and are more vocal about sharing ideas for innovation. They are more promotable and often discover that foodservice management is a rewarding and exciting career shift or second (third, fourth) career. However, these employees often have higher expectations of their managers and the companies they work for, especially if they come from a more regimented and/or regulated industry or line of work. They are knowledgeable about compliance and what constitutes good management practices; they will not tolerate a weak or inconsistent manager, which may result in more complaints and grievances.

The evolving and escalating expectations and responsibilities of HR executives precisely mirror those of any top executive. The successful HR executive must be passionate about being a lifelong learner, striving for excellence in every aspect of performance, being able to measure and prove his or her value to the company, knowing the ins-and-outs of our business as well as an operations manager, talking the language of the candidate and the employee, seeing the world through the eyes of candidates and employees and managers, being an expert at translating the impact of regulatory and legal developments on your world, and being a master at strategizing, selling, advising, and shaping processes and outcomes. Good HR management is good business management.

Key Takeaways

- It is not enough to know the important trends in your industry. Instead, you must have a firm grasp of the industry itself to relate to and communicate with potential talent and discern whether each is a good fit for the job.
- Building a strong leadership pipeline is critical.
- Active candidates may provide volume, but passive candidates are frequently where we find that rare exceptional talent. Cultivating passive candidates takes time and patience, but the rewards are worth it.

- Use technology both for your professional improvement and to improve your communication. HR practitioners are lifelong learners, and it is imperative to read everything you can to continue developing talent in your company.

- It is important to build rapport with potential candidates. By identifying with them, relating to them, and sharing the details of the job—including the good, the bad, and the ugly—you are more likely to understand them, and they will understand you.

- Generic e-learning can be useful for basic skill developments such as sexual harassment or diversity training, but for more personal, nuanced skills, one-on-one mentoring groups and small, interactive groups are far more beneficial.

With more than twenty-five years of human resources experience, national vice president of human resources, Kareen M. Muros, SPHR (senior professional in human resources) stands by her maxim "Good HR is good management, and good management is good HR." To be an effective strategic business partner, Ms. Muros understands that HR is not limited to administrative and compliance oversight. Attracting top-notch talent, fostering effective employee relations, mitigating legal and regulatory exposure, and encouraging solid performance management are critical to building and retaining successful world-class teams. Ms. Muros is a strong advocate of HR's responsibility to enrich the workplace through highly visible diversity and inclusion initiatives.

Prior to relocating to Tampa, Florida, Ms. Muros had eleven "glorious" years at the Rose Garden Arena/Rose Quarter, home of the National Basketball Association (NBA) Portland Trail Blazers, in Portland, Oregon. In 1996, she headed the Cutting Edge Concepts (a Paul Allen-owned Portland Trail Blazers/Oregon Arena Corporation company) human resources department. Her oversight extended to the startup of the Washington State Exposition Center and (then) Seahawks Stadium in Seattle. She was retained by Ovations as director of HR following the January 2005 lender acquisition of the Rose Quarter and was promoted to national director of HR in July 2005, supporting Ovations' forty-two sports and entertainment venues and 6,000-plus employees throughout the United States and in Canada. Her oversight has now grown to support one hundred-plus facilities and more than 8,000 employees in the United States and Canada. Ms. Muros was promoted to vice president of human resources for Ovations in January 2007.

Ms. Muros has twenty-five years of HR, training and development, labor law, and management experience in sports and entertainment, manufacturing, and technology, for national and international companies. She earned her BA cum laude from the University of California at Santa Barbara, and graduated summa cum laude with her MS from the Georg-August Universitat in Germany and Pepperdine University Law School. Muros has been recognized for her contribution to workforce development initiatives in the Northwest (Oregon and Washington), as well as for her contribution to professional development and certification programs for HR practitioners, at-risk youth employment programs, and innovative learning programs. She continues to take an active leadership role in developing and implementing programs designed to foster individual and team success in the workplace.

Inspiring Employee Happiness in a Generationally Diverse Workforce

Beth Jacobson

Director, Human Resources

Office Environments of New England LLC

ASPATORE

Introduction

Currently, I am the director of human resources (HR) at Office Environments of New England, a position I have held for almost four years. I began my career in HR twelve years ago, when I worked in the financial services industry for a private equity firm, where I was thrown into an HR role and had to learn HR from the ground up. I spent a number of years becoming proficient in the intricacies of labor laws, benefits, plan administration, employee relations, and all the other aspects of HR.

From the financial services field, I transitioned into the health care field as the director of human resources at a small, non-profit, regional hospice for one year. After a year, I was approached about a terrific opportunity as the director of HR for the subsidiary of a global furniture manufacturing organization and jumped at the chance to work for Office Environments of New England.

Office Environments is a unique organization. Fundamentally, we are an organization that specializes in creating environments for people to work, learn, and collaborate in. We seamlessly integrate commercial furniture, audiovisual technology, and architectural products to create customized spaces that enable our clients to meet specific business goals.

Office Environments is a regional dealership with three locations in Massachusetts, one location in New Hampshire, and approximately 175 to 200 employees. We are a wholly owned subsidiary of Steelcase Inc., one of the nation's largest global furniture manufacturing companies. We are unique in that we are the only dealership Steelcase wholly owns and have the particular honor of being its representative "model" dealership.

Steelcase is a benevolent parent who supports us wholeheartedly by allowing us to do what we do best, which is sell integrated solutions and services—furniture, audiovisual products, architectural products, project management and design services, move services, etc. We are quite different from the classic commercial furniture dealerships that sell chairs and modular workstations, and we have unique challenges because ours is a sales, service, and high-technology business.

Managing Talent for Success

We have a strategy we call the ADDR strategy—attract, develop, deploy, and retain. It is our objective to institute ADDR to its highest level, which we measure using an annual employee satisfaction survey. Among our many survey questions, we ask our employees if they would recommend Office Environments to their friends and colleagues as a great place to work. Our goal is to achieve at least a 90 percent level of agreement on this statement.

Our talent management practices have evolved greatly in recent years to accommodate various market changes. Because we are a sales organization, we have to be exceptionally responsive to the market. Our products and services are constantly changing in reaction to the market's demands. Our budgets and profitability drive much of what we are doing for talent management. We are always adjusting and fine-tuning to ensure that we are getting the best results for our money.

In terms of attraction of personnel, we are fortunate to have a built-in attraction for recruiting—our offices. As we are furniture, audiovisual, and architectural product integrators, our offices are a living, physical example of how a prototypical workspace works. Our workspace is our biggest attraction for recruiting and has a mesmerizing effect on candidates. But it is HR's role to ensure that we hire the right people for the job and not allow them to be sold on the glamour and glitz of the office.

HR is also highly focused on people and developing their individual abilities, which differs from other departmental objectives that may focus more on sales results, product knowledge, services, and deliverables. From an HR perspective, we are deeply concerned about our employees' success and that they are maximizing their potential. We want to ensure that we provide them with the relevant training and development they need to achieve and grow. Such an approach aids in our employee retention. We are a small company, and we strive to utilize a high-touch, customized approach wherever possible. I personally know everyone in the organization, and I want all employees to feel they can come to me individually with questions, issues, and problems if they need to.

Our department managers play a significant role in our talent management because they are responsible daily for executing our organizational strategy. As the managers of our employees, it is incumbent upon them to develop and deploy their people, to make sure that they are moving forward, that they are learning, that they are growing, and that they are staying challenged and engaged in their work. HR cannot accomplish this on a daily basis. HR can supply our managers and staff members with the tools they need, but ultimately our managers are responsible for evaluating, making recommendations, and keeping their staff engaged and productive.

Communication Practices

Good communication throughout the company enables our talent management to remain effective. We are always talking, sharing ideas, brainstorming, and ferreting out needs and objectives. We have an executive management committee that meets monthly where we talk candidly about what our problems are, what issues we are facing, how we can help each other, and how we can resolve any issues that may exist.

From the executive level, we take it down to departmental levels. I speak to managers all the time. My job is extensively involved in employee relations, helping managers manage their people and working with them. We have an active open-door policy at Office Environments because we want people to come and talk to us. If employees do not feel they are getting resolution from their immediate supervisors, we empower them to ask questions and to speak out because the objective is not necessarily to follow the hierarchy, but to resolve issues in the most productive manner possible. This approach works for us and encourages an open and collegial atmosphere within the organization. We are not encouraging our staff to subvert our managers, but we do encourage respectful debate and discussion on issues to achieve the best outcome possible. Often resolution cannot be achieved; however, our employees know they have the opportunity to escalate an issue and be heard.

One hallmark of our organization is our monthly town hall meetings. All our employees are invited and encouraged to attend, though attendance is not required. The meetings are held monthly on a Thursday afternoon, and we serve beer, wine, hors d'oeuvres, and munchies. Our managers report on the progress of their departments; we show the most recent company financial data; and we talk about bookings and trends, who our top ten customers for the month were, our profitability, and our backlog. Then we outline progress on our marketing initiatives and what events or activities we are sponsoring. Our employee satisfaction team announces any upcoming events. HR introduces new hires to the employee population, length-of-service awards, and programs or training opportunities. We celebrate our successes and examine our failures or lost opportunities.

These meetings are open, relaxed, fun gatherings, and we encourage people to ask questions and create a dialogue. The president, the senior vice president of sales, and the chief operations officer/chief financial officer (COO/CFO) are present to take any questions. We have lockboxes where people can drop in questions if they do not feel comfortable asking them in a group setting, and the leadership answers the questions at these meetings. We try to hold at least three of our monthly town hall meetings in our Wilmington, Massachusetts, location so our field and operations personnel have an opportunity to participate, as well. We also hold a full-company annual meeting at the beginning of each fiscal year, where we review the financial results of the previous year and unroll our updated strategies and objectives.

Managing a Flat Structure

Previously, while I worked in the financial sector, the corporate structure leaned toward the classic hierarchical establishment. Office Environments is different; it is a much flatter structure. This flatness is exceptionally challenging in a large sales environment where we are moving huge volumes of products and services that require strict adherence to certain policies and procedures to maintain profitability.

Our historical inclination is to allow individual creativity in developing cost-effective solutions so our sales force can maximize its earnings; yet we still must adhere to standardized business practices to maintain product and service integrity. This presents a real internal struggle for us. There is a delicate balance between achieving customer satisfaction and remaining highly competitive while at the same time maintaining accountability in a business environment. In a flat structure, if you do not have strong policies and procedures, bedlam can result, with each individual attempting to maximize his or her own potential. We work for a balance to make the structure flexible and allow it to bend and move as much as we can while adhering to the policies and procedures that keep us profitable and productive.

Trends and Technology

In HR, we always have to be aware of trends when formulating and revising talent management strategies. Outsourcing and variabilizing talent is a trend that is affecting many businesses today, as is technology. One of the biggest trends, though, is generational diversity in the workplace. Never before have we had four generations in the same workspace. We are creating environments that serve all four generations and environments and work spaces that will address the different work habits in each of those generations, while working and appealing to all of them. Mobile workers and telecommuting are also trends to watch.

Office Environments is not a particularly high-tech or cutting-edge environment; however, we are all on e-mail and use computers and BlackBerrys. We strive to be sparing in our use of paper in our office and communicate primarily via e-mail. From an HR standpoint, we have changed with technology, too. We now do open enrollments online, and we administer all our benefits electronically. Our communication with employees is largely electronic, which is much faster, more efficient, and more accurate.

Even our training is delivered through technology. We have a large audiovisual department and service our client base with video technology and streaming technology. In the last two years, HR has videotaped all our organizational internal training, and we now have an on-demand training department where new employees can go onto our company intranet and access steamed video training. We utilize a proprietary platform that merges the videotaped image with the actual PowerPoint slide presentation to create a seamless tutorial. Now, our staff members can access these tutorials at any time from any location company-wide.

The feedback from the employees and the managers has been terrific. Employees can view video whenever they want, and we are freeing up managers' time by not requiring they personally brief every new hire. Streamed video, as a training tool, has been instrumental in elevating the overall knowledge base of our employees and ensuring a consistent message is delivered repeatedly.

Budget and Talent Management

In a tight economy, HR benefits and services are usually among the first budget items cut. My budget for talent management encompasses about 30 percent of my overall HR budget. The recession has forced us to shrink our financial footprint to remain competitive and grow strategically for the future. We are constantly being forced to become creative in operating within a smaller budget, such as variabilizing costs or in our implementation of streaming video and other technologies for training, which are lower in cost.

The economy has had a tremendous impact on talent management. We had to lay off a little more than 30 percent of our staff in 2009. Our particular business follows market trends by about six months, so we have been hit a little later in implementing our cost-cutting solutions. The good news is that we are now seeing an uptick in business interest and activity, and we are much more optimistic, as is much of the country. For the future, business is getting better—there is no question of that. Regretfully, our fortune-telling skills are limited to the big picture, so we cannot tell how fast or exactly when we will have recovered from this recession. Currently, our people are working at maximum potential, as we have been extremely conservative about adding back staff until our backlog has stabilized and we are clearly able to identify a trend.

On a more positive note, the slow economy has resulted in many opportunities to show our people how much we care about them and how valuable they are to the organization. We thank people much more and show our gratitude whenever possible to let them know we appreciate what they do. Because this is a fundamental practice of good business, it is a shame that it has taken a recession to bring us back to our roots, so to speak. Simple appreciation is such a fundamental tenet of job satisfaction, and we strive constantly to embed this into our culture. With our current financial constraints, we simply do not have the money to do everything we would normally like to do—spot bonuses, gift certificates, and so on. But our organization, at the very least, is nothing less than the sum of our people, and we strive to honor that daily by making sure our people know that we do care and appreciate them.

One of the smaller programs we implemented to help our employees adjust to the economic downturn was a formalized mentor program for key employees. We selected ten employees and paired each with a senior manager for one year. It gave our staff members immediate access to senior leadership and their guidance during this rough time that they would not have had otherwise. Since we had not had a previous mentoring program established, this program was started on a small scale with no budget or financial allocation. With had only ten mentor-mentee pairs, but we spent considerable time and effort matching people appropriately, trying to make sure that we had structure around the program and support for everyone involved. It was received well, with good feedback. All the participants appreciated it and found value in the experience. We are continuing the program with a new group this year, but still on a small scale. Because our structure is so flat, it is hard to do a mentor program with such a limited number of senior managers, but we are determined to keep it in balance.

Facing the Generational Challenge

Engaging each generation in our workplace is fundamental to HR's business. A primary tool we use to embrace this engagement is the physical structure of the workplace itself—the desks, chairs, offices, etc. Office Environments has the most exciting and dynamic offices I have ever seen. They are simply exquisite. We have leveraged Steelcase's studies of the workplace and insights into generational work behavior to create a cutting-edge application of office furniture, audiovisual equipment, and architectural products in our Boston workspace. Few organizations can claim what we have in our space, including the latest in technology, video conferencing, and flat-panel technology.

We are also an early adapter of green technology, such as our state-of-the-art lighting system that equalizes luminosity throughout the day to maximize the ambient light from our windows. Our physical environment directly addresses the four generations at work and establishes areas that maximize their creativity and productivity. While our general floor plan is open, we allocate space for individuals to work privately or collaboratively, as needed. We have varying types of meeting spaces and technology to enable different types of work, whether it is teleconferencing, showing slideshows, using spreadsheets, or displaying drawings or designs. Even our staff café is bright, open, and airy, with floor-to-ceiling windows that can be shielded to enable presentations for up to eighty people.

Our workforce is always changing. The average age of our employees is approximately forty-two years old. More than half of our employees have been with us ten years or longer. These people will retire within the next ten to fifteen years, so we are working to bring in the next generation to take those places.

We are also working to keep our baby boomers current with technology and social media. We have some amazing Gen X and Gen Y employees who know how to do everything with technology. They manipulate technology faster and better than our boomers; yet our boomers have the industry knowledge and interpersonal skills that are lacking in the Gen Xers and Gen Yers. Consequently, we are striving to create an atmosphere and environment for knowledge transfer to make it exciting and fun for all the generations, which also maintains engagement in the organization at the same time.

It is not only technology that Gen X and Gen Y bring to us; it is their connection. They are worldwide—they are truly global networkers—more so than our boomers and traditionalists, who tend to function more as regional and local networkers. But our boomers are true relationship builders. They are all about the one-on-one interactions, taking people out for drinks and dinners, and developing the personal relationship, which turns into the business relationship, which then turns into a long-term experience for both the client and the company. The boomers are teaching those interpersonal skills to the Gen X and Gen Y employees, who tend to be more linked to their computers and e-mail addresses than individuals. We are witnessing the cross-pollination of knowledge—the Gen X and Gen Y employees teach the boomers how to open the doors, and the boomers teach them how to walk through.

Determining Success

It is important to determine the success of talent management. We use performance reviews, but more relevant measures are employee turnover and employee satisfaction surveys. Those give us our true measure of effectiveness.

If employees are happy, challenged, engaged, and growing, they usually do not leave the organization. Even if employees complain, they are engaged and working toward betterment. They want things to change, and they care enough to say something about it. Complaints are not bad things. Fundamentally, they are requests for help and action. When an employee doesn't care enough to complain, then I know he or she has become disengaged and will either leave or, worse, become a negative or destructive force in the environment. When that happens, things truly are not working and need to be fixed immediately.

In HR, you have to constantly stretch your creative muscles and be on the alert for new ways of measurement. You can ask the same question only so many times until the answers become meaningless. We cannot rely on one specific area for measuring our successful talent management programs; we have to continuously measure ourselves against not only our past performance but also other industry competitors and companies.

We are quite fortunate, with the advent of technology, that we are no longer mired so much in benefits, administration, and compensation. HR is now a strategic partner, sitting at the table, in helping the business grow and move forward, but HR is also being looked to as the creative inspiration for change, as the source for creatively managing the generations in the workplace without alienating them. We are showing managers how to build loyalty with their staff, which will be one of the biggest challenges going forward.

Key Takeaways

- Remember ADDR in your talent management strategy—attract, develop, deploy, and retain.
- In a flat management structure, you must have strong policies and procedures in place so you can balance the required policies with

customer and market demands to remain flexible, pliable, and nimble.

- Look for creative approaches to manage and engage the various generations in your workforce.
- Complaints are not bad. As long as people still care enough to talk, they are still engaged. It is crucial to maintain two-way communication and transparency.
- Gen X and Gen Y employees are particularly adept at global networking and making connections. Baby boomers are particularly adept at building strong, one-on-one relationships. Use your multigenerational workforce to teach each other and balance these skills.

Beth Jacobson, director of human resources, joined Office Environments of New England LLC in 2006 as the human resources manager. With more than twelve years of experience in human resources and administrative and operational management, she is responsible for the management of the human resources and facilities departments and oversees recruitment, benefits, compliance, policies and procedures, safety, training, and employee relations.

Previously, Ms. Jacobson was the director of human resources for Old Colony Hospice in Randolph, Massachusetts, and the human resources officer for Nautic Partners LLC in Providence, Rhode Island. Her experience also includes administrative and operational management positions in the financial services and non-profit sectors.

Ms. Jacobson holds an undergraduate degree in management/leadership from Northeastern University.

Think Strategically, Act Tactically

Michael Zimmerman
Vice President, Human Resources
Shore Health System

ASPATORE

An HR Leader's Role

I have worked at Shore Health System, a division of the University of Maryland Medical System, for nine years. Shore Health comprises two of the University of Maryland Medical System's eleven hospitals. As the vice president of human resources (HR), I am responsible for all HR activity within these two hospitals. This role includes overseeing such diverse areas as training and development, organization development, occupational health, our child development center, wellness, ethics, and spiritual care, as well as the traditional areas of HR—recruitment, staffing, compensation, benefits, employee relations, and performance management.

Developing a Comprehensive Approach to Talent Management

We take a comprehensive approach to talent management. This process starts with our first point of contact with an employee—when someone applies for a job and goes through the recruitment process—and continues with on-boarding, personal development during his or her career, and performance appraisal.

Several years ago, we created a model designed to define a set of competencies for successful individuals in this organization. To do so, we considered extensive input from management across various disciplines, as well as professional literature and national benchmarks, to determine what these competencies should be. For example, we do behavioral-based interviewing that emphasizes a particular set of competencies. Our management team decided these seven were critical to success in our organization:

- Service orientation
- Building relationships
- Initiative
- System thinking
- Developing vision
- Teamwork
- Organizational commitment

Those competencies are woven into the employee orientation process once an individual is hired, all of the standard training and development processes, and, finally, the performance evaluation system. All of this helps ensure our talent management takes an integrated and comprehensive approach.

Evolving Talent Management Practices

Initially, our talent management practices were somewhat limited to managerial development. Over the years, we have expanded this range to include staff employees' first-line supervisors and individual contributors. We have also expanded the opportunities for training and development to the extent that we now have one of the best orientation processes for new nurses in the country. Not only have we received awards based on these processes, but we've also been written up in several publications for them, and we have presented the concept at multiple conferences.

We call our in-house clinical orientation program for new nurses coming out of nursing school "Critical Care University." Rather than just placing them into a job with a few days' orientation and hoping they will succeed, we actually continue their education for about nine months and weave in some extended instruction. We then gradually put them on the floor to take care of patients, so that the transition from student to active patient caregiver is smoother and more gradual. These new nurses also have mentors to help them through the process.

We also didn't begin with succession planning. That was added as the program evolved. The bigger concern in succession planning for us, however, was middle management, not senior executives. So we drove succession planning down to that level of the organization, and we concentrate on promising line staff who exhibit the potential to be developed into middle managers.

The Importance of Re-Evaluating Competencies

We make a point of re-evaluating competencies from time to time to make sure they remain current. Generally, the list of competencies from which we select our "core" doesn't change, but organizations do—they grow, and their cultures evolve—so we want to make sure our competencies are still relevant.

Most recently, we have been evaluating outside partners to automate and manage our talent management process for not just our two hospitals, but for the entire University of Maryland Medical System. As the executive sponsor, I am overseeing the selection process; in fact, we are in the final stages of vendor selection at the time of writing this chapter. Once we select a partner and complete this project, we will have truly integrated selection, orientation, on-boarding, and performance management processes—all of which will be automated.

The Roles of Other Executives and Departments

Other executives and managers are instrumental in defining the competency set we use. They give input on what those competencies should be, and they help with the development of on-the-job training programs and succession planning; in fact, several of these executives are on the selection committee for our succession planning program.

We also just created a learning committee that will review all our organization's learning needs and call attention to any gaps. Once we have agreed on a need and approved the implementation of a program, we decide on the structure: classroom training, on-the-job training, computer-based training, or whatever is appropriate. All these actions are led by the learning committee and succession planning committee, each of which comprises members of the executive and management teams. They all make important contributions to our competencies and talent management processes.

Enabling Collaboration and Communication

We have quite a collegial team; turf is not an issue here. I think everyone on the management team truly understands the value of what each person does. Our two hospitals are relatively small community hospitals. Most hospitals of our size do not engage in the kinds of activities we do. I think our management team realizes the value of our talent management initiatives and that our processes set us apart.

For example, we are also a Magnet-designated health system—an important designation in the nursing world. The Magnet Recognition Program was developed by the American Nurses Credentialing Center to recognize health care organizations that provide nursing excellence. Worldwide there are only 372 Magnet facilities at the time of this writing, so this designation truly does set us apart. Part of the process of becoming a Magnet facility looks at collaboration and shared governance. We could not have achieved this distinction without demonstrating a collaborative culture. We have a collaborative approach throughout the entire organization. Shared governance is the norm here.

HR Trends

Information technology drives much of what we do in HR. Over the last ten years, information technology has created systems that can enhance the effectiveness of talent management tremendously. Not only do these systems influence our effectiveness, but they also enhance our efficiency. It is important to make this distinction. That we do something efficiently does not necessarily mean that the outcome will be effective. However, it is difficult to do anything effectively that isn't at least moderately efficient. The two are intrinsically related, but they do not always accompany each other. Information technology's development, however, has helped in both regards.

Also, over the past decade or so, human resources and the rest of the business world have come to an understanding regarding the effectiveness of organization development activity. Once upon a time, organization development was viewed more as a fluffy "nice-to-have"—and consequently, was one of the first areas to be cut in difficult times. Now, when I talk to professional recruiters, I note that there are many HR executives coming up through the organizational development world. If you look at job postings, you'll see that many of the HR executive positions require a background in organization development. There has been a significant shift in recognizing the importance of this function.

Quantifying a Return on Investment in HR

Unfortunately, return on investment (ROI) in human capital is difficult to measure. It *can* be measured, and there are benchmarks available, but they are not common measures on many business scorecards. We measure the human capital ROI by looking at the hard costs associated with human resources and the investments we make in our people compared to our bottom-line income. I think measuring the return on our human capital, along with our investments in more traditional "hard" capital, is valuable. It helps demonstrate, in language business people understand and appreciate, the value of our people. For anyone who is more data-oriented or financially oriented, it gives them at least a modicum of understanding as to what the value-add is for talent management activities. You do, however, have to have a longer-term view. The return may not be realized for years. Succession planning is a good example.

We are non-profit, but in the for-profit world especially, quarterly and annual statements are key: *what* we did this quarter, *how* we did this year. For good reason the annual report is critical for many companies to show return on investments. The return on human capital investment, however, may take three, four, five, or more years. When calculating the ROI on human capital and the investment in talent management, it is not a quarterly or annual measurement; you have to look beyond that. We have taken a long-term strategic view and recognize the value-add that talent management activity can create into the future, not just over the next year.

Using Technology: Increased Efficiency and Effectiveness

We are in the process of implementing a much more efficient and effective applicant tracking system and on-boarding process. The HR information system needs to be linked to applicant tracking, so data entry is done only once: the user enters it in one place, and it populates everything downstream, which is much more efficient than doing data entry multiple times. The technology allows the single input to flow downstream wherever it is needed.

The application of competencies should be populated automatically in a performance document, so there are no files in a cabinet. Succession planning is part of that system, as well, so positions at least to mid-level management have back-ups designated. These back-ups are evaluated in their readiness to fill the position, so we have bench strength and are much more proactive than we used to be when preparing for retirements and replacements. If we don't have anybody to fill a position, we know that right away and can start targeting potential individuals and giving him or her developmental opportunities.

The Effect of the Economy

The economy hasn't had as much of an impact on our talent management strategy as might be expected. It has clearly affected our bottom line, but talent management is a long-term strategy. The economy is cyclical. In terms of practical application, we have experienced a slow-down in recruitment, as well as some lay-offs, which is unusual in our world. We suspended our nurse orientation program for one semester because we are not hiring, so the classes are not needed. In that sense, the economy has indeed dramatically affected our tactical implementation. However, our overarching strategy is still the same. The economy fluctuates, and it will eventually change and improve. When it does, we have everything in place to pick up where we left off.

The Importance of Mentors

Most mentoring programs are fairly traditional. Select individuals are assigned to or matched with a mentor, such as those we are targeting for advancement and people in the succession planning program. Consideration should be given to whether the mentor and person to be developed will be a good fit. Some mentoring programs in the past were more arbitrary in their mentoring choices—executive A mentored potential executive candidate B—and not much thought went into whether they would be a good match on a personal level. Companies now put more into assessing whether the match is a good one because if the individuals don't mesh well, the mentoring relationship won't work as it is intended.

Good mentoring programs define the mentoring relationship better than they did in the past. Matching personalities for a good fit as noted above is one example. The Army actually did mentoring before many businesses did, and many businesses tried to adopt that model. The model worked well for the time in which it was conceived, but over the years, we have learned it needed some adjustments.

For example, the process needs to be time-defined. We tell mentors they will engage in this program for one year, and at the end of the year, they are welcome, but not required, to continue with the relationship. In the past, it was up to the mentor or person being developed to end the mentorship, but this posed a challenge. How were they supposed to end their mentoring relationship gracefully, without offense or hurt feelings? To resolve this, we now give people an automatic out, which I think is important, as the relationship will change over time.

In non-corporate mentorships that come about naturally, one of the most interesting—and counter-intuitive—observations is that frequently the mentor-protégé relationships end badly. This situation is actually quite common because the protégés come to feel that they are on a more equal level with the mentors, or that they have learned all they can and are ready to move on, while the mentors may feel that the protégés still occupy a junior role. Even worse, the mentor may come to see the protégé as a threat as the protégé gains knowledge and experience. While this outcome can be sad in life, it can be a disaster in the corporate office. We want to prevent this naturally occurring conflict. Defining the point at which the relationship will end helps avoid this, and it reassures both parties that it is appropriate for the mentorship to end at some point.

The Roles of Employees as Individuals

We have a wellness program in which we assess health risks and create a program for the individual based on his or her needs. We offer in-house wellness initiatives, such as weight loss programs, yoga, Pilates, smoking cessation, and even belly dancing. Overall it is a pretty traditional program (well, maybe not the belly dancing), with a focus on the individual.

As part of our HR strategic plan, we just created a diversity council, which addresses generational differences, as well as the more traditional diversity. I am much more interested in diversity of thought. Where diversity programs add value is in the different ways of looking at an issue—the varying experiences each unique individual brings to the table. The surface differences are superficial. The real value is in the underlying thought process and experiences we all have that help create an open, mutually respectful environment for everyone.

We have made a conscious attempt to assemble various viewpoints from different departments so that the entire organization is represented. It is a diverse group that represents ethnic differences, racial differences, and generational differences, as well as gender and alternative lifestyles. This body's charge is to help us formally identify what things within the organization we need to be sensitive to in order to make everyone feel welcome and accepted. They let us know if we are being naïve or inadvertently insensitive in any of our words or actions, and they help us identify possible issues in everything from the tactical (a marketing poster) to the mundane (cafeteria food), so that we can enhance the entire concept of diversity within the organization.

Forecasted Changes to the Workforce

The challenges in our workforce are largely based in the geography and the culture of this region. While we are only ninety minutes from major urban centers, including Washington, D.C., our actual location is in a rural area. We also have an older workforce. Three of the counties we serve have an over-sixty-five age population of between 18 percent and 21 percent.

With a small and older labor pool to draw from, we often must bring individuals to the area or "grow our own." Our nursing program has been particularly helpful in this respect. Our changes in the workforce will concentrate on diversifying our organization. To this end, we are apt to make some changes to benefits programs and various other tactical HR initiatives to foster this diversity.

Key Advice for Any Future HR Executive

It is vitally important to make sure that your talent management strategy is comprehensive and integrated. One program doesn't create talent management; nor do multiple programs if they are not functionally integrated and philosophically compatible. The entire business strategy has to flow and be integrated with the principles of talent management. If done piecemeal, you get almost no value-add, and maybe even redundant expense. There is, however, a huge value-add to be gained in the synergy of the pieces. When you put them all together in a comprehensive, integrated plan, the sum of the whole is greater than the parts.

Additionally, make sure the talent management strategy fits the culture of the organization. Different organizations have different cultures; take the textbook strategies of talent management and mold them to fit your organization's culture. I coined a phrase: "Think strategically, but act tactically." That is critical. An HR executive needs to think strategically, but then act tactically—be able to put the theory into practical application. Don't become so enamored with the textbook, or the theory, that you lose sight of the real desired outcome—to make your organization better, not to add another HR program.

Key Takeaways

- Take a comprehensive approach: Begin the talent management process from the first point of contact with the employee (in the hiring stage), through the employee's exit from the company. Use a variety of sources to create a competency model, and then use this model from the employee orientation stage through training, development, and employee evaluation.

- Encourage company collaboration: Bring executives together to encourage a variety of perspectives with regard to company strategy (such as defining competencies). Furthermore, make use of an integrated variety of programs to help transition and develop employees.

- Rethink and reevaluate competencies: Because organizations grow and change, check that your competencies are still relevant to ensure a productive and efficient business.

- Take advantage of new resources and opportunities: Stay abreast of trends in technology to help maximize both efficiency and effectiveness.

- Think strategically, and act tactically.

Michael Zimmerman came to Shore Health System as vice president of human resources in August 2001. His experience in both the for-profit and the non-profit worlds brings a depth of business acumen to his academic beginnings.

Previously, Mr. Zimmerman served as vice president of human resources at Western Maryland Health System in Cumberland, Maryland, from 1997 through 2001. He also served as senior human resources consultant/director of education and development at Alliant Health System in Louisville, Kentucky, from 1995 to 1997. Prior to 1995 Mr. Zimmerman served in several management positions with Sprint Corporation.

Mr. Zimmerman received a master's degree in industrial relations/personnel administration from Saint Francis University in 1989. He received his bachelor's degree in humanities education from Pennsylvania State University in 1975. He is married with two children.

Talent Management for Total Employee Engagement

Betsy Mitchell

Vice President, Organizational/Staff Development

Green Bay Packers

ASPATORE

Introduction

My role as vice president of organizational/staff development is new to the Green Bay Packers (2008) and unique in professional football. When our leadership changed in 2008, our new president was committed to ongoing leadership development and to a strategic approach to our business, which is crucial to supporting our overall goal of winning championships.

I had been an independent consultant to the Packers for seventeen years. My initial work with them was to provide mental health consultation to players dealing with the challenges of the National Football League (NFL). I did this for more than ten years while maintaining a private clinical practice and developing a management consultation business.

In 2003, the Green Bay Packers' business was transformed by the renovation of Lambeau Field from a ten-day-per-year venue to a 365-day-per-year destination. This required transformation of the leadership roles, and I was asked to work with the leaders of the organization to expand leadership and management capabilities. This role has expanded over the past several years, and I am now responsible for human resources and employee relations, strategic planning and deployment, and leadership and management development. I am privileged to work with the whole organization, including all departments, with my focus being individual and organizational development and goal achievement to drive business results.

The Role of Individual Goals in Talent Management

The renovation of our stadium dramatically changed our business operations in 2003. This resulted in a huge shift in our businesses to accommodate having customers in our building and businesses every day and not just on ten game days per year, as had been the case since 1957, when the stadium was built. With this change came expanded and added staff duties, responsibilities, professional opportunities, expectations. We have developed new talent management activities to support these business needs and continued to expand our efforts in leadership development throughout our organization. We are committed to linking every employee to our strategic plan and having full alignment and engagement of everyone in working toward our True North goal of "striving for championships while being guided by our values."

Our talent management is directly connected to our strategic planning process. One of our core objectives is "promoting excellence across all organizational areas," which includes initiatives related to best-in-class workforce development and leadership development. We have engaged every employee in aligning with our strategic plan by establishing individual goals that directly align with one or more of the five core objectives defined in our strategic plan. To meet these individual goals, each employee has a personal development plan that is linked to our performance management system (an appraisal system that utilizes various competencies as measures).

Tying all of those pieces together is a recently implemented incentive plan that allows us to offer financial incentives for different levels of performance. When conducting a performance appraisal, we look at our baseline expectations, as well as the individual goals each employee sets with his or her manager for the year. If the employees meet or exceed the performance expectations, they have an opportunity to financially benefit through our incentive plan. Although we conducted performance appraisals previously, we did not tie the results (attainment of employee goals) to any incentive. This has just been developed in the past two years.

We provide ongoing learning opportunities for individuals and departments throughout the year. They can take various assessments to determine their areas of interest and/or need for skill development. We share opportunities for enrichment with all employees and have a training budget dedicated to employee growth and development. This affords access to development programs as they come up during the year.

As vice president of organizational/staff development, I oversee the process of talent and performance management and compensation, which is managed by our human resources (HR) department. My position is new to the organization and signaled a big change in emphasis and allocation of resources. This change has allowed organization-wide initiatives for cross-training and ongoing development, thus offering many opportunities for employees to learn from each other across internal departments, as well as from external experts. All compensation and bonuses are overseen by organizational/staff development and HR. These efforts are collaborative with the directors of all departments in the organization.

Roles of Executives and Departments in Talent Management and Succession Planning

Executives and their departments have direct responsibility for what happens within their departments and the business results achieved. They work as a team to constantly direct progress toward achievement of strategic initiatives and goals. The leadership team in our organization consists of the senior staff (five vice presidents and the president) and the directors (eight department heads). This team considers organizational needs and what it will take to meet them with a strong emphasis on talent development and retention.

Though our brand is recognized worldwide, we are a relatively small business with approximately 200 full-time employees. Because we can't offer much vertical career movement, a key challenge for us is retaining our top talent. As a result, we have to look at other ways to manage and incentivize the development of our people. We are currently doing individual assessments to discover what interests our employees have and to find ways to cross-train them for other positions and shared responsibilities. This is all part of managing our talent as we plan for the future.

Our succession planning involves identifying the key roles for each department and exploring ways to build lateral strengths in the organization by tapping into people from other departments who may have talents and interest in those areas. We then cross-train them to promote internal communication and relationships while concurrently building organizational capabilities. For example, we have cross-trained security personnel to work in the facilities area on non-game days. These employees are doing similar things in terms of function, but have different focal points or rationale for their roles. We are keenly aware of the need to be prepared with succession planning and are instituting training in the areas where we have a strong need for operational back-up. We are not doing this to the extent that we would like, but we are moving forward and intend to engage leadership succession planning in the near future.

Building Collaboration across Departments

To further underscore our cross-training commitment, there are many informal opportunities for our employees to connect with each other. For example, every Friday we invite all employees to lunch and encourage them to connect with people outside their own departments. A more formal example is how we use multi-departmental project teams to drive our business. We draw people from different departments together to work as team members on specific projects (social media, stadium signage, etc.). This allows us to offer other ways to develop leadership and management talents. We offer leadership opportunities that may not result in position or title changes, but do afford our employees great experience in working across the organization to build alliances, problem-solving capabilities, and collaborative skills that are essential today. To further promote this collaboration, we have monthly meetings in which leadership team members share their team's work with the rest of the organization. This reporting out is a time to celebrate success, promote increased communication, and strengthen vertical and horizontal relationships.

During these meetings and others, we assign teams additional projects and request updates on current ones. We have an internal communication system where we post continuous updates on various projects, news items of importance, and other happenings that involve our employees. It is there that you might find the employment anniversary date of someone or a notice of the birth of a child or an event for employee involvement. This allows people in the organization an opportunity to support, congratulate, and assist others. We are trying to promote connections for people outside their immediate areas and enhance relationship-building and collaboration with cross-functional teamwork.

Upcoming Employment and Technology Trends

We are dealing with many issues right now related to the economic situation and the changing generational profile of our employee pool. We are acutely aware that people come to us with different work styles and ethics, and we are always looking for ways to turn these differences into strengths, rather than struggles for the organization. We believe these differences work to our advantage because they broaden our ability to interface with our fans who hail from all generations, backgrounds, and cultures.

We are also assessing the impact of recent technological advances on our business and on our fans. We recognize that we are in a world of immediacy, yet have the challenges of all businesses with workflow, managing expectations, and handling these demands. We are using technology to our advantage in many ways by offering online access to our employees for various evaluations and assessments and external online access to select departments. I think this is standard in most places now.

We are also using online technology for benefits administration. Our employees can independently access their benefit packages. This is quite new for us. We encourage people to participate in online learning opportunities, which might include understanding their benefits and selecting continuing education offerings for self-improvement and fulfillment of personal goals. We use some of the same technologies to research best practices and benchmark our progress.

Challenges

One of our major challenges in talent management is our employees' range of capabilities, which is not surprising, given that they range in age from fifteen to eighty years old. While technological challenges sometimes become obstacles, most of the time they are opportunities for connecting and supporting each other in our quest for excellence. We have a great deal of confidential information about employees and our business, so we always have a concern about what level of protection we need with our information. We are well equipped with an exceptional information technology (IT) department, and we continue to handle the challenge of balancing confidentiality and progress.

We feel the challenges of many companies as we try to maximize our talent through collaboration and training across disciplines. This is something we did not have to attend to much in the past, but the economic and technological changes of today make it important. We are looking at employee engagement and retention even though our turnover is minimal. We have a high number of employees who have been with us for many years (on both the administrative and the business sides of the business), which is somewhat unusual. This might be partly because we are a highly regarded professional sports team that attracts people to this nice place. There truly is no better sports venue than Lambeau Field!

Having employees develop and grow is challenging from the resource allocation perspective (i.e., time and money). If we had unlimited ability to tap into those resources, it would, of course, be easier. However, in the end, we usually find ourselves wanting to do more, yet having to deal with the limitations of time. There is only so much time available in an eight-hour day (even if we try to squeeze ten hours into eight). We also have some small departments with one or two people in them serving key functions. We have a hard time having others fill in for these people, which limits their availability to things that take them out of their areas. We are working on this challenge by tapping other people in the organization and by engaging part-time assistance.

Employee Development

We are committed to ongoing development and education, as evidenced by the fact that we link training directly to each employee's yearly individual goals, on which part of their annual incentive is based. We live in an area with only two universities and one technical school within thirty miles. The overall educational offerings are somewhat limited, so we encourage e-learning for continued employee development. This includes Webinars, online conferences, video conferences, and more. We have just entered a partnership with the University of Wisconsin-Madison for extended learning and networking opportunities with other companies, which we expect to be a great development program. We also have a tuition reimbursement program in which we work with an employee interested in pursuing higher education to tailor a program that enhances his or her skills and builds capabilities in our employee talent pool.

Many of our employees are licensed by the state in their professions (including our electrician, attorneys, health care staff, and others). We support all the mandatory training needed to maintain active licensure with financial and time reimbursement plans. We also require training in risk management for people in high-risk areas. We offer and encourage cardiopulmonary resuscitation (CPR) and automated external defibrillator (AED) training for everyone, and it is required in a few areas.

We recognize the importance of mentoring in individual professional development. Although we have not yet developed a formal mentoring program, we encourage employees to seek others internally and externally who can offer them support and expertise. One way we encourage internal connectedness is to offer lunches for our staff on Fridays in which they are expected to seek those co-workers whom they do not see regularly. They are willing to share their areas of expertise, and we encourage cross-generational and cross-departmental engagement. For example, we ask our employees who are savvy with computers to offer assistance to those who are not. We have an intranet site in which social, developmental, and educational offerings are posted to promote employee interactions. One of our HR department's goals this year is to develop and implement a mentoring program, and we are looking forward to moving that along.

Work-Life Programs

We are fully committed to promoting health and wellness for our families and our employees. We have a highly successful Wellness Program called PULSE. At least once each month PULSE features some interactive activity that is designed to help people think about how they are taking care of themselves and the impact of simple, small changes on their overall health. For instance, PULSE developed programs to help increase activity by starting a walking group at lunch, a group to do yoga after work, and other events to increase physical activity. In addition, our paid time off (PTO) policy is quite flexible and generous, allowing employees to take time to spend at family events (a core value of ours) or the activities of their communities and homes. We offer other fun activates throughout the year for employees and their families. These are a highlight for many of our folks, and we see the value extend far beyond the physical changes they might make to the relationships they may add to their support networks.

Sometimes families and individuals have difficulties. We support our employees and their families with an Employee Assistance Program in which we have professional mental health assistance available to them within twenty-four hours of their calls. This program is for all our employees, is totally confidential, and is fully supported for the first four visits by our organization. Our employees have utilized this effectively and report being very happy with the availability and assistance they have received. The feedback we have received indicates that the program has helped many employees deal with internal and external stressors that were affecting their overall performance and work relationships. This is a preventive approach to life issues that we believe proactively precludes longer, more disruptive problems. For many, just knowing this is available at no cost to them is reassuring and increases the likelihood that they will get the help they need.

Having time at home and being away from the office can be especially positive for some of our employees, and we do everything we can to support the balance of work and home. The use of mobile devices that allow remote access to e-mail, the Internet, and phones can be helpful. They can also create a problem of never being "really off." We suggest they monitor their off-site availability and take care not to be totally linked in when they need to be away and taking a break from the stressors of work. Here again, we look at the blessings and the curses of technology and continue to go back to our basic values. We believe in promoting families and a healthful lifestyle, so everything comes back to moderation.

Embracing Diversity in the Workplace

Working in a small northern city for a major professional sports franchise allows our workforce to experience cultural differences in many ways. We have football players and coaches coming here every year from all parts of the world with every possible background. We have employees of all ages (15 to 80). We have people of different religions, cultures, genders, races, and levels of talent. We naturally view our differences as strengths that enhance our overall organization and team performance. For a sports team, the concept of differences adding to the overall success of an organization (or a football team) is a common analogy. We pointedly and consistently send clear messages about who we are, our values, and how we do business with the underlying theme always emphasizing honor and respect for all.

There is an acronym we use that spells out the PACKERS WAY, which defines the expectations we have for everyone in treating each other and our guests. We promote tolerance and understanding and the celebration of our differences and strengths. Every spring we have an all-organization meeting in which all the coaches, the administration, and the employees are assigned to group mixers and activities that help them understand the importance of everyone in the overall success of our team. Thus, the person responsible for painting our building may spend time with our head coach in a one-on-one conversation learning about who they are and developing a personal relationship. We are insistent about the "little things" in our environment that promote engagement and a feeling of being valued, and this goes for everyone at every level. It is all about relationships, a theme that resonates loudly at Lambeau Field. We believe relationships are key to maintaining and developing people by fostering a desire for full engagement. They are part of our talent management strategy, and, more importantly, they are essential to defining who we are.

Measuring Success of Talent Management Strategies

We measure the success of our talent management strategies by looking at goal attainment through quarterly reviews with our employees, achievement of business results utilizing defined metrics, and employee surveys and interviews. Each employee has defined development goals that are reviewed and adjusted every quarter with full evaluation at the end of each fiscal year. We look at development needs extensively during the budgeting process, where the entire employee pool is assessed to determine what talent needs we have, where we need to expend resources for further development, and what adjustments need to be made for the next fiscal year. This is where senior staff leadership is essential.

For effective and successful talent management, senior staff must support initiatives at every level. HR must demonstrate the importance of aligning the talent management process with overall organizational strategies to demonstrate added value. They are responsible for demonstrating a return on investment and the impact on business results as benchmarks of success. A challenge here is that metrics for business results are generally more objective and easily defined than growth and development goals, which can be subjective or completion-based. This can lead to difficult conversations around balancing resources (time and finances), which need to be held early and often to ensure that everyone is aligned and supporting both employee and business growth.

In an aligned strategic planning process, all initiatives drive toward achievement of core objectives. When objectives or initiatives tap the same resources, strategic decisions are made at the senior staff level that may not easily cascade down through the organization. This requires consistent and positive communication to maintain full employee engagement, which is crucial for talent retention and employee satisfaction.

We are strongly committed to leadership development and have a major initiative to develop our existing and emerging leaders this year. We believe everyone in our organization is a leader regardless of title. We actively acknowledge that leadership development is a key component of talent management. Our overall strategic direction (True North) is the ultimate goal for everyone in the organization. All our objectives support True North, and our employees have a keen sense of direction and purpose, knowing what they do is integral to attainment of that vision. Winning on and off the field is what drives us all.

HR is integral to the success of our talent management programs. It has broad organizational connections and is able to promote the message of empowerment that comes with opportunity for personal growth and development. Utilizing performance reviews, employee development plans, and other offerings is helpful in getting people excited about opportunities. The more people we have involved, the greater the potential affect for continuous improvement. Ongoing talent management and learning are unifying experiences for many, with benefits far beyond simply adding skills or capabilities in an organization. They add to a culture of openness, tolerance, and collaboration that, although not easily measured, can have broad impact for organizational success.

Key Takeaways

- Individual goals that align with the company's strategic plan are established for every person in the organization.
- Succession planning involves identifying the key roles for each department and building lateral strength by cross-training people from other departments who have the talent and interest in these areas.

- Collaboration can be built across the organization by encouraging the formation of teams that are drawn from different departments to work on special projects (social media, etc.).
- HR needs to demonstrate the importance of aligning the talent management process with overall organizational strategies and demonstrate how talent management supports business results the organization is trying to achieve.

Betsy Mitchell, an eighteen-year member of the Green Bay Packers, began her third year as the organization's vice president of organizational/staff development in 2010.

Named to the then-newly created position by Packers president and chief executive officer (CEO) Mark Murphy July 23, 2008, Ms. Mitchell is responsible for all employee relations, professional development, strategic planning and deployment, and leadership and management development, as well as the human resources department. The bulk of her previous experience with the Packers was as the staff and player development consultant.

Ms. Mitchell has a master's degree from the University of Wisconsin-Madison and is a state-licensed mental health professional with more than twenty-five years of experience in private practice.

In her first role with the team as the staff and player development consultant, which began in 1993, Ms. Mitchell utilized her counseling and leadership-development skills to better the organization by providing players, coaches, other Packers staff and their families with consultation services on issues of performance, life circumstances, and leadership. She worked to develop optimal relationships between members of the team and the organization.

Through her career with the Packers and prior experience in private practice, Ms. Mitchell has had the opportunity to present for and consult with the National Football League (NFL) on all areas of player development, conduct policies, and leadership initiatives. In addition to her work with the NFL, Ms. Mitchell's seminar and presentation experience includes the American Medical Association, American Psychological Association, Wisconsin Clerk of Circuit Court Judges Association, Wisconsin Bureau of Training and Standards, American Nurses Association, Wisconsin Nurses Association, and Wisconsin County Police Association. Ms. Mitchell previously owned Mitchell Management Consulting, which specialized in performance and organizational development, program design, and performance enhancement for small businesses. She also designed and developed behavioral medicine programs and previously owned and managed a private behavioral care practice.

In the community, Ms. Mitchell is a member of the First United Methodist Church, a board member for the Greater Green Bay Community Foundation, a board member for Cerebral Palsy Inc., an advisory board member for the Wisconsin Sports Development Corporation, and a board member for Woodlawn Cemetery. In February 2010, she was recognized by Green Bay's Bay Business Journal as one of its "People You Should Know" for her significant impact in her field, as well as her exemplary representation of the greater Green Bay community. She also was a finalist for the American Foundation of Counseling Services Ethics in Business Award for 2009.

Born in Tomahawk, Wisconsin, Ms. Mitchell grew up in nearby Minocqua, Wisconsin. She was married for twenty years to Pete Mitchell, a lieutenant with the Brown County Sheriff's Department, until his death in 2003 from colon cancer.

Ms. Mitchell has two children—a son, Aaron, twenty-seven, who graduated from UW-Madison law school and practices intellectual properties law in Chicago, and a daughter, Emily, twenty-five, who also graduated from UW-Madison with degrees in history and economics and currently is attending Marquette University Law School. In her spare time Ms. Mitchell enjoys traveling, hiking, fishing, reading ("everything and anything"), word games, music (mostly vocal), and spending time with family and friends.

Using Talent Management Strategies to Maintain a Successful Organization

Roger J. Sheets

Vice President, Human Resources

Woolrich Inc.

ASPATORE

Introduction

I am the vice president of human resources (HR) for Woolrich Inc., an apparel and fabric company that involves both marketing and manufacturing. Woolrich has the distinction of being the oldest apparel company in the United States, beginning in 1830. We still manufacture in the United States, but we also source product all over the world. In fact, we are one of the few companies in the clothing and textile industry that still manufacture in the United States.

My background is in the classic areas of HR—recruiting, training and development, labor relations, and compensation/benefit areas, and in organization development and strategic planning. I am certified through the Society of Human Resource Management (SHRM) as a senior professional in human resources (SPHR) and teach that program as an HR course at Penn State University so that other people can become certified. I am on the board of directors and am a past chairman of the board of the IMC Corporation and am a past president of the Manufacturers' Association of Central Pennsylvania. I am also a board member of the Workforce Investment Board for the state of Pennsylvania and past chairman of The American Apparel and Footwear Association Human Resources Council.

Organizations are defined by the employees within those organizations. Successful organizations have successful employees who feel confident and comfortable in their jobs and are not threatened by the loss of their jobs or by management. Employees need to feel a part of the innovation and change of the organization and a part of the strategic planning of the business and help in those processes. When efforts are directed toward developing the best programs and involving employees in the processes of innovation, change, and strategic planning, the organization will continue to move toward success. Talent management plays a key role in that movement toward success.

Hiring and Retaining the Best People

At Woolrich, talent management starts with hiring good people and then retaining them; you cannot hire good people and then let them walk out the back door. To make sure we hire the best, all our hiring managers must complete a training program that covers how to recruit, interview, and ultimately hire the greatest talent. All the managers and vice presidents have taken a course in behavioral interviewing. Essentially, anybody in the company who interviews has to complete this program, whether they are hiring hourly employees or managers.

While behavioral interviewing techniques are an important focus of this program, we also cover what you can and cannot ask an individual and the legal ramifications involved in the interviewing process. Another key element of the recruiting process is the sourcing of candidates. To compile the most qualified pool of candidates, Woolrich utilizes a broad range of nationwide recruiting sources, including social sites such as LinkedIn, database search programs, recruiters, institutes of higher education job boards, and local media sources.

Once you have the best people employed, it is important to retain them through training and development, competitive pay and benefits practices, and fair and consistent supervision and management practices. When employees see that you are spending the time, effort, and money to develop and manage them, it will have a positive effect on retention rates. Further, we place great emphasis on wellness and health. We run various events, including health fairs and wellness programs, and encourage family members to participate, as well. We also have a fitness center on-site that our employees utilize at no cost. We are located in a small, rural area where families know each other, so we encourage that interaction and promote the importance of family orientation and involvement.

One of our interesting programs is called "Leaders Developing Leaders," which, despite how it sounds, is actually not a mentoring program. We assign two managers to each vice president, who is then responsible for the development of those two individuals for an eighteen-month period, and the vice presidents have truly taken ownership of this program since its implementation seven or eight years ago. We give evaluations to all the participants in this program (including the vice presidents) after the eighteen months are over, and I am always pleased when I hear people confess that they did not know what the vice president did before taking part in their program, or when they say they have a better appreciation for what another individual does in his or her department. We originally designed our Leaders Developing Leaders program to break down barriers between departments and disintegrate the silo effect, so I am especially pleased to see comments of this nature. However, the program is also about developing people, and it has in many ways constantly evolved since its inception.

After the eighteen months are up, we assign the vice presidents two new people. A couple of the managers have even been promoted to vice presidents themselves, so they get to complete the program from the other side. There is not a great deal of technology or paperwork involved in this program; it is hands-on, and each individual takes his or her role and responsibility seriously, which is why it works so well. It is intended to be a learning process for both parties.

The reason we do not call Leaders Developing Leaders a mentoring program is that some of the managers in the program are older and have been with the company longer than some of the vice presidents they might be paired with. In a mentoring program, you typically think of a senior person taking a younger employee under his or her wing, but that is not the case here. It is mutually beneficial and has a great impact on improving our retention. We also do many activities with this group of participants; for example, we have dinners, attend Penn State football games, and have tailgating parties, so the group feels appreciated and valued.

A Team Effort in Developing Talent

As a result, executives and other departments contribute to developing our talent management strategies. For example, when we assign the vice presidents to two people, many of the vice presidents bring the managers to their staff meetings and give those employees the opportunity to truly learn the other side of the business. We also take our president and vice presidents off-site for three or four days every year to discuss talent management and succession planning, as well as business and strategic issues and how we can further expand our program.

We also have a group of forty managers with whom we conduct an annual strategic planning session. The process begins with a confidential survey about the strengths of our company, weaknesses, opportunities, how well they think we work as a team, how well they think management works together, what the company will look like three years down the road, etc. I collect that data and have a session first with our president and staff, and then with all the managers. It is interesting to see the developments people talk about from year to year from a strategic standpoint. All these managers have input and participation in the strategic planning process, and I think that involvement and communication is important. We also have the vice presidents present at the sessions so that we are all collectively providing feedback.

Our talent management practices continue to improve. Ten years ago, we did not have a great deal of focus in this area, but in the last seven or eight years, I started putting substantial effort into developing our talent. Fortunately, the economy has not had a significant impact on our talent practices. Although the economy may affect things from a growth standpoint, where perhaps in a better economy we would have grown a bit more, in terms of financing our programs, it has not had a major effect overall.

The Benefits of Generational Diversity

There are people in our Leaders Developing Leaders program with generational differences, which also helps in keeping each generation of our workforce engaged, and they do learn from that. We have a lodge on our premises that we use for many endeavors, such as training and development, as well as for dinners and parties where we can bring people together to socialize.

Generational diversity is important for the success of our company because our product is outdoor clothing. We do not make clothing for a twenty-year-old, a fifty-year-old, or a sixty-year-old; we make clothing for the outdoor enthusiast, whatever age that person is. Having people who are in various cultural areas is important to us because that is to whom we sell apparel—everybody, not just one particular age group. Having people who are older and younger on our merchandising teams is important to meet the needs of our customers. It is also important to us as a business and to our company from a cultural standpoint.

Planning for Future Success

Succession planning is also important to us. At our offsite meetings, the president and I sit with each vice president and discuss the employees in the organization who should be on the replacement chart. We develop these charts and include who is currently in the position, who will be ready in one to three years, and three to five years, as well as any immediate high-potentials who could replace each vice president right away if necessary. It is a three-way discussion with open dialogue. For instance, a vice president may feel one employee is right for his replacement, but we may disagree. The president or I may know something about that person that would keep him from being able to do that job. Once we decide on the individuals, we also discuss what needs to be accomplished in terms of development, and if that cannot be accomplished, then we consider another person. It is vital that the people involved have open and honest dialog about potential candidates on the replacement chart.

Three years ago, our chief executive officer (CEO) passed away of a massive heart attack in our fitness center at the age of fifty-four. His death was sudden and unexpected. We were able to maintain a sense of order because we implemented our succession plan, naming our chief financial officer (CFO) as the replacement. Many companies have succession planning, but it is all a paperwork process; they do not usually discuss those things openly. You must know who is next in line for the position before a position opens, not after the fact; otherwise, you run down a path of confusion and uncertainty.

The other aspect we discuss in our succession planning is what happens when people retire and take their knowledge with them. Whom do we have who also possesses that knowledge, or whom can they transfer that knowledge to? The replacement chart is only one piece of the succession planning process; if you stop there, then you miss the whole point. The idea is that you need to retain knowledge within the company. I have seen situations where four or five vice presidents retire within the span of one year and take their job knowledge with them. In many ways, the company has to start over. Someone needs to be in place who can receive that knowledge transfer.

Our Leaders Developing Leaders program also addresses this need. We are trying to transfer information back and forth within the organization and department so that when someone does leave, he or she does not leave a big knowledge hole in the organization. It is not only the succession of people that is important, but also the succession of the knowledge those people posses.

Measuring the Success of Talent Management Programs

To measure the talent management programs, we look at retention, conduct surveys of job satisfaction in departments, and perform organizational development programs. For example, we go into the merchandising and design department, which is a group of twenty people, and talk about the employees' different personalities using the Myers-Briggs personality inventory, for example. We follow that up with team-building exercises to determine the team's strengths. Everyone rates how good they think the team is on a scale of one to ten (one being low), and typically they will say the team is a six or seven. We then look at the competitive environment we are in to see where we need to be—typically it is a nine to ten—and then discuss how we get there. We break them down into groups and have each group work on ways they think will get us where we need to be, and then we come back together and discuss them. We list them all on the board and let them vote to select the top initiatives. Typically, we have everyone commit to the top initiatives and follow up in the subsequent months to check progress.

Conclusion

Talent management is a continuous process that involves everyone. It begins the day you start thinking about a job you need to have done. Now is the time to think about talent management. First, you need to think about whether you will replace that person and keep the job as is or enlarge it, make it more interesting, or make it a better job or a stronger job. Then you need to think about where you can get the people who are the "A" players to do that job and what you will do to retain them.

Talent management spans from the day a person comes into the organization to the end, when that person retires or moves on; it is all those pieces. However, it takes a great deal of hard work and effort; it does not just happen. You have to know your jobs, think about the jobs, and know how to pick the best people you can find for each job—and then retain them. Talent management continues throughout the life of the company. The strategies for talent may change, but the concept remains.

Key Takeaways

- Talent management starts with hiring good people and retaining those people.

- It is important to break down barriers between departments to further facilitate training and development. Pairing vice presidents with lower-ranked employees can create transparency, encourage collaboration, and strengthen your succession planning efforts.

- Generational diversity can be as important as cultural diversity in the overall success of a business—especially with regard to knowledge transfer.

- Knowledge sharing and succession planning are critical to the future success of any company. Having the people in place is only one piece of the puzzle; you must take the time to plan and make sure a knowledge transfer takes place.

- Talent management is a continuous process that involves everyone in the organization. It is not an HR program that can come and go.

Roger J. Sheets is the vice president of human resources at Woolrich Inc. Mr. Sheets has a BS in business administration from Southern Illinois University. He attended the Manufacturing Management Program (MMP) at Harvard University, and Walter Mahler Associates, Succession Planning and Accomplishment Analysis.

Mr. Sheets's professional affiliations include board membership in the American Apparel and Footwear Association, the Manufacturers' Association of Central Pennsylvania, the State of Pennsylvania Workforce Development Corporation, and the IMC Corporation. He also serves as an instructor in human resources at Penn State University.

Employing Collaborative Practices and Development Programs to Meet Tomorrow's Needs

Holly Shoener Sharp

Vice President, Human Resources and
Environmental, Health, and Safety
Insituform Technologies Inc.

ASPATORE

Introduction

I am the vice president of human resources (HR) and environmental, health, and safety. I have been with the organization approximately six years and in my current role for the past two years. Insituform Technologies® Inc. is a leading worldwide provider of cured-in-place pipe (CIPP) and other technologies and services for the rehabilitation of pipeline systems. Insituform's businesses consist of sewer, drinking water, and energy and mining pipeline rehabilitation and protection.

Proactive Talent Management Strategies

Our talent management strategies have several components. These include succession planning, talent assessments, and a robust recruiting strategy.

We engage in our succession planning process for senior-level roles annually to identify gaps and to define strategy for how to address an unplanned vacancy at the senior level so that we maintain continuity in the business. In this process, we evaluate our interim strategies for filling that particular position, as well as any recruiting or external sources we can utilize to find supplemental help until the position is filled permanently. We have been tightly focused on putting clear and concise developmental plans in place for the candidates for senior-level positions, and we meet with them semi-annually to review those action plans and ensure that they are gaining the skills necessary. At the senior level, we address our international positions similarly.

Ensuring that we have the appropriate bench strength for our key management positions is a top priority for us. Our board of directors is keenly interested in the executive-level successor plan, as well how we would fill these positions in an emergency or urgent situation.

We also have a talent assessment process for our field-management ranks, which is geared more toward developing those individuals for senior-level roles in the organization. Since these positions are the building blocks for our organization, a field manager can take several different career paths. We strive in the talent assessment process to provide the foundation skills, experiences, and competencies to enable those field managers to be eligible for upward mobility across that range of career paths.

Finally, we have a robust recruiting program that includes a strong internship program. The internship program endeavors to bring in either entry level field engineers to fill project management roles or corrosion technicians and engineers for both our sewer and water and energy and mining segments. Our internship program makes a substantial effort to partner with universities and schools to recruit talent into the organization.

Our talent management practices have evolved in the past several years. The key is being diligent in pre-planning and understanding the needs of our growing organization. Our talent management is absolutely a collaborative process between operations and human resources. My boss— the chief executive officer (CEO) of the company—and I, of course, discuss the overarching strategies. However, to implement these strategies, we work closely with the business unit leaders (i.e., the senior vice presidents and general managers) to identify their needs. The business unit leaders have a clear ownership stake in the talent management practices, as they must commit time and resources to train and develop talent.

The Role of Technology in Tracking Progress

Our tracking technology has enabled us to monitor progress in our succession planning, recruiting, and developmental activities over time and has demonstrated how we have been able to improve with respect to time to fill positions, quality of placements, and retention. We also have electronic training and development systems, so now we can manage our efforts with much more sophistication and ensure that people are adhering to our development processes and giving them the attention they deserve. Of course, from a practical perspective, most of the training assignments are hands-on learning activities.

Committing Resources to Talent Management

The business unit leaders allocate resources for training and development directly into their budgets. As we move into 2011, we would like to increase funding for the internship program because that is truly where the "rubber meets the road" in growing and developing our bench strength. In the last several years we have received strong executive support to increase both the talent assessment and the internship programs, which has made a positive impact to our bench strength.

Our company is fortunate that we have been growing over the last several years. This situation has opened additional opportunities for our key performers, and we have been able to sustain and grow our internship program. Fortunately, we have increased our level of commitment in that direction based on the fact that our industry continues to grow.

Foreseeing Future Trends

We need to establish two sets of goals (shorter-term and longer-term) and fully understand the company's overall direction, plus the outlook for each business unit. For example, if you know from working with your business leaders that you will experience great international growth (in Asia, for example), you need to be planning for that well before vacancies are created. This can be a challenge because obviously you don't want to add overhead costs to your organization until you know that you have the work or that you are definitely moving into those areas. However, if you have done the pre-planning, when the key turns, you know which steps you are going to take.

In the next five years, I believe we will experience more international growth across the business, and we will be challenged to develop a candidate pool that is internationally mobile and desirous of international assignments.

Moreover, one trend we need to watch concerns differing generational expectations. Some of the college graduates we are recruiting have different perceptions about what constitutes an acceptable work-life balance and the speed in which they expect to progress within the organization. This has been an eye-opener and a challenge for a number of our team members.

You need to be aware of such generational issues when you introduce new talent or college graduates into your company. Helping the management group understand generational differences is key—both sides of that equation need to be able to understand and work with each other because our tenured employees have tremendous institutional knowledge that must be passed on to the younger generations to ensure we grow the organization in the future. Once managers understand what makes each of the generations tick, they have an easier time managing those employees.

When considering the topic of work-life balance, we need to be cognizant of some of the generational differences, and we need to help new hires understand what the position's time commitment expectations are. A construction project-oriented environment is not an 8-to-5 classroom situation, so new employees need to be prepared for what their work will actually look like. We try to do that by providing realistic job previews and expectations for them. On the flip side, we also understand that people need to take vacation time, so we strive to ensure that everybody is able to take the paid time off they have available.

Several benefits we offer seek to address work-life balance, including gym memberships and our wellness program. We also encourage people to participate in other fitness activities, like marathons and walking events. These types of activities help their overall well-being.

Our employee population is geographically and culturally diverse. We have approximately 3,000 employees worldwide.

HR's Role in Developing and Executing Talent Management Practices

From the HR team perspective, we are focused on formulating the methodology and training the business unit leaders on implementing talent-management practices. For those practices that are more field-management-oriented, the field HR team actively works with the general managers to deliver that process and compile the results. My corporate HR director and I are directly involved with the succession planning that is executed at the corporate level for the senior team members.

Education and Training Initiatives

We utilize a learning management system (LMS) to deliver a great deal of quality training electronically. These trainings are in the areas of core competency and skills development. The system has been beneficial to us;

even though our organization has sites in many geographic regions, we have still been able to effectively deliver training. The LMS and some of our training classes have definitely appealed to the younger generations, so we try to maintain a balance between classroom training and all-electronic training.

Some of our skills-based training programs are mandatory for our project-management group. Training for the core competencies is more closely tied to the developmental plans we put in place through the succession planning or talent assessment processes.

We also utilize mentoring programs in certain of our business units. For example, the Corrpro group instituted a mentoring program that has been successful for engineers and corrosion technicians. The program provides each mentee with practical experience, a learning/developmental plan, and a mentor to counsel the participant, with the focus on becoming fully successful in a new role or growing into a stretch assignment. This program is scheduled to be expanded in 2011 across our other North American business segments.

Overall, I believe we have made great strides in our talent management practices. Because several of our business units have unique cultures, we have to be sensitive to the cultural nuances of those particular areas when we put their talent management plan together. Organizationally, we have found that it is not our training methods that change, but, rather, the type and extent of communication about the programs and what the organization is trying to accomplish through the programs.

Challenges in Developing and Implementing Talent Management Strategies

One of our biggest talent management challenges is to invest the necessary time in training entry-level individuals. Because we are so geographically diverse, many offices are quite small, and there is a single person trying to train an individual and continue to perform his or her own full-time job. We are now looking at alternatives to this scenario, such as setting up centers so the interns can work out of a particular location that houses several resource trainers. But the Catch-22 to this situation is that we like to introduce interns to areas where we have need for future growth, so it is not always easy to train them in one state and then transfer them to another. This is a dilemma.

The key to managing talent is that it has to be a collaborative effort, and the business units need to feel ownership of the program. It is sometimes too easy to make HR fully responsible for talent management or succession planning when the reality is that we can guide the process and make recommendations, but the buy-in has to be at the business-unit level.

Key Takeaways

- Effective talent management involves being diligent in pre-planning for future needs and understanding how the organization is growing.
- HR must develop interim strategies to address unplanned senior-level vacancies to help maintain continuity within the business.
- Generational differences between workers are palpable, but once managers understand what makes each generation tick, they will have an easier time.
- Managing talent has to be a collaborative effort; the business units need to feel ownership of talent-management and succession-planning programs.

Holly Shoener Sharp joined Insituform in September 2004 as director of human resources for the Affholder Tunneling division. In 2007, she was promoted to senior director for human resources and environmental, health, and safety for Insituform. She holds a Bachelor of Science degree in engineering from Penn State and a Master of Human Resources degree from the Keller Graduate School of Management. Prior to joining Insituform, Ms. Sharp was the director of labor relations for Rental Service Corporation, a North American construction rental company.

Acknowledgment: *Yvonne Tedder, director, human resources.*

Collaborative Leadership and Bridging the Generation Gaps

Deborah K. Hoover

Director, Human Resources

The Urban Institute

ASPATORE

Introduction

Currently, I am the director of human resources (HR) for the Urban Institute, which is a nonprofit, non-partisan public policy research organization based in Washington, D.C. We conduct research in a range of topical areas—everything from education, health, and tax to justice and child welfare issues. We also do technical assistance work overseas in developing countries. It's important to note that although we are a not-for-profit firm, much of our funding is derived through government contracts, thereby influencing much of our decision-making and many of our systems and processes.

I have been employed with this organization for almost thirteen years. Prior to that, I was a visiting professor, did a bit of consulting, and served as director of HR for a small title insurance company in New York City.

Talent Management Strategies

Our talent management strategies are predicated on the need to attract and retain elite policy researchers. They are highly sought-after graduates from some of the best universities in the United States and typically have career opportunities available to them in the private sector, academia, and government. Ultimately, we are focused on building a culture that appreciates and sustains intellectual curiosity, entrepreneurship, and growth.

Clearly, the strategies we employ for junior researchers are different from those we use for more senior types of positions. At the junior level, we're sensitive to the kind of culture necessary to nurture and mentor young talent, also commonly referred to as the "millennial knowledge worker" (which is sort of the buzz word of the day). Accordingly, we recruit aggressively from excellent policy programs, provide numerous developmental opportunities, and quickly reward skill acquisition in this group.

At the senior level, talent management is more of a challenge because we need to cope with competing demands on those senior researchers' time. Not only do we want and encourage them to participate in recruitment and outreach efforts, but we also want them to mentor younger staff, conduct their own funded research, and still have time for their own professional development. Balancing these priorities and satisfying this group's needs means we must provide them better project and time management tools, support some time that can't be billed to external funders, and respect their desires for impact and influence.

Finally, we also need to recognize that our administrative talent has to equal our research talent for this organization to be successful. Administrative units need staff members who possess top-notch competency in their own fields, as well as the communications skills, confidence, and productivity to win the respect of the research staff. Because these employees come from a range of industries and have skills that are transferable more generally to other organizations, recruiting this talent can be quite challenging. Accordingly, we've poured more effort into retaining this talent once we've found it. Our turnover rate for this group is quite low, and I attribute it to a number of institutional attributes—our more collaborative and relaxed environment, a competitive salary and excellent benefits package, and jobs here that are challenging and rewarding. Here, administrative professionals can feel as though they, too, are part of the national policy world.

This organization's overall success is highly dependent on collaboration among all three of these groups—junior and senior researchers and administrative professionals. Consequently, we must design and integrate our strategies so that compensation practices, HR policy, training, and all we do address the need to support collaborative behaviors and take into account generational needs, as well as personal and professional needs. I will admit that we struggle from time to time in this area, and I don't think we're alone. For a smallish organization, it is particularly difficult to address the needs of multiple employee groups and design strategies tailored to each. In the end, I feel as though we are continually challenged to be fair, transparent, and mindful of the allocation of our resources that we devote to any one group.

We have been in business for a little more than forty years—in fact, most of our senior-most talent grew up here—so the issue of succession planning is a burning one currently. In Washington, D.C., and in our industry, we've not seen a labor downturn or recession in the sense that other people have seen, and the competition for our talent remains huge because we are competing with universities, government, and other research, contract research, and non-profit research organizations. However, we, along with our sister institutions, are not immune to the demographic trends facing the U.S. workforce and therefore are trying to adapt and change in response to all of these trends—but perhaps most important are the effects of the aging workforce and the retirement of the baby boom generation.

Our talent management practices have evolved over the past five years to account for some of these forces—though probably not as quickly as they needed to. In our industry, it was a much kinder, gentler world ten years ago; it was a much more collegial kind of an industry, where we enjoyed a more open relationship with other firms. You partnered on work, and people moved in and out of these organizations in a less competitive way. However, in the last five years, our world has gotten much more complex, and our competitors are much more aggressive. Consequently, our talent management practices need to reflect that change. We need to be faster. We need to be more decisive. We need to recognize that we're in a business; even though we're a not-for-profit, it is still business. Being mission-driven isn't enough. We must become more responsive, more proactive, and more strategic at a time in which it is extremely difficult to take a step back and gain perspective.

Role of Other Departments in Talent Management

It is incumbent on our research practice leaders to be partners in developing our organization's talent management strategies. HR cannot do this by itself; it is not strictly an HR initiative. As much as I might want HR to lead in sourcing talent, developing our brand, and building compensation and benefits programs to retain staff, these are not ultimately HR's decisions alone. Our leaders need to be a part of the conversation because these are overall business decisions. They need to agree and help implement these strategies because they feel they are the strategies that will help make them successful, too. Also, because we have quite a collaborative environment, it is not my position to explicitly direct them. Instead, my approach is to use whatever influence I have to build coalitions of people who agree on an idea or a need and can help drive the initiative forward.

To facilitate collaboration and communication between departments, we use e-mail, an applicant tracking system, and other technology tools, but electronic communications are simply not enough, even though people are inclined to use them the most. There's still nothing that takes the place of going to someone's office and having a face-to-face meeting, especially about how one will address a talent management issue. Whether we're talking about a recruitment effort, a compensation issue, or an employee relations problem, I prefer to uncover data that supports an idea and bring it to a group of people who have the ability to effect change, get them onboard, open the matter to a wider set of people, and then develop an action plan for implementation.

However, to formulate and devise the best talent management policies and procedures, you need to know yourself first—yourself as an organization. Far too often, we overestimate our own capacity to train people, to mentor people, and to nurture people. We tend to overestimate the patience and resources we have to do those kinds of things. I think we're far better off if we recognize our own limitations, learn to love them, and build our plan after we recognize them—which, in truth, can be quite difficult to accomplish.

Staying Abreast of Technology and Other Trends

We are a small organization that is composed of approximately 300 regular staff and a few hundred other people who are either consultants or local country nationals whom we hire in host countries. We use technology for our applicant tracking systems, data systems, and HR record-keeping systems, and we are using more and more technology like Facebook, LinkedIn, and Twitter. Although we do not yet have an integrated, strategic effort in place for these areas, we are organically headed in that direction.

It's worth noting that I haven't mentioned at all performance management. Although those sorts of automated systems would enhance our talent management capabilities, I'm mindful of our resource limitations. For now, we will continue to use written assessments (self- and supervisory-appraisal) that addresses goals and achievements, but they are not particularly well designed for uncovering development needs across the organization. In addition to resource limitations, we must also be mindful of what makes sense for an organization such as ours.

For example, our talent management staff—i.e., our recruiters—have known for some time that we need to get onboard with social media, but, again, we're considered more of an elite think tank. We haven't had to go out and hunt research applicants much, even at the junior levels. At the senior levels, it is always more a matter of personal networks, which, again, means recruiters haven't had to work terribly hard at developing applicant pools. However, we are increasingly aware that we need to stay relevant and stay informed of technology and social media developments. To maintain our brand as a firm that uses data and technology to further its work, we in HR also need to adopt technological tools our staff would expect of such a firm. So, for example, in the coming weeks we will try "tweeting" a note about a difficult-to-fill position and revise our profile on LinkedIn.

I stay abreast of other talent management trends in several different ways. I read as much as I can, and I talk to my colleagues in the HR world—especially the ones in my industry. They may not have the best, latest business jargon to describe what's working, but they have real hands-on experience with respect to what our organizations can adopt. I also talk to many consultants. Although we do not actually engage consultants regularly (we are not that big), simply maintaining a conversation about various trends can be invaluable. Additionally, we do not do much in the way of outsourcing, but I still find opportunities through networking to speak to consultants who are ahead of the curve in understanding talent management, and I often get ideas from them that can be adapted to fit our organization in whole or in part.

Economics- and Generation-Based Challenges

In the think-tank world—and definitely in D.C.—some funding streams are not as readily available as they once were, which has affected our fund-raising efforts. Government contracting money is still available, but we do feel the strain when the other sources—e.g., private foundation money—are less readily available. The mix of funding we receive, whether primarily private grant or government contract, has a fair amount of influence on our recruitment posture and how we compete with others on compensation matters. Washington's unemployment rate has stayed fairly low relative to the rest of the country, which also puts some pressure on salary growth. For instance, some of our sister institutions reported last year that they did not award any salary increases, but now I think we're all scrambling to deal with the fact that our talent is highly sought after—and they will not stay put without good compensation and benefits. Because the economy remains a concern, compensation decisions are particularly difficult at this time. Unfortunately, salary survey data tells you only what has happened in the past, and after last year's experience, I'm not sure I will be putting much stock in survey data reporting salary budget trends.

Here at Urban we are also experiencing an organizational generational shift. We have many individuals in their later years who are looking toward their future retirements, and the next generation behind them in their late forties and early fifties is wondering what the organization will look like when they are managing the Institute. The biggest change, therefore, that we will need to address is the aging and retirement of our leadership and how we identify, support, and develop this next generation of leaders.

While some of our staff has remained very engaged as they approach retirement, others have seemingly taken a mental vacation. We need our people to be engaged all the way to the end, which is a problem we will be grappling with for some time. However, to begin to address this challenge, we've started a series of initiatives that focus on three main ideas— identifying future leaders, supporting future leaders, and developing leaders. For this, we've turned to performance appraisals and current research leaders for information on who the future stars are and what development needs they possess. In addition, we've turned to the next generation, formed a working group on this topic, and have asked them directly about their developmental needs and the supports the institute provides. In all, this approach incorporates a repeating theme here—collaboration and engagement with multiple-employee generational cohorts.

Once upon a time, bridging the generation gap was not a point of focus, but in the last few years, I have seen more and more discord or disconnects between the generations, so efforts in this area are becoming increasingly important. For example, e-mail and other kinds of technology are great from one generation's standpoint, but not from another's. Although I'm not the type of person who says you shouldn't use a tool if it's available to you, I think there is a serious over-reliance on e-mail and not enough emphasis on engaging in face-to-face dialogue and building interpersonal skills.

Additionally, we see a difference in work styles and ethics between the generations. Often supervisors have expectations about how subordinates should be behaving (e.g., calling in for time off, using electronic devices in meetings, responding to work requests, feedback frequency) that are simply not in sync with more junior staffers. What seems commonsensical to older employees cannot simply be taken for granted, and supervisors are often reminded they must make explicit some of these basic work-style requirements to build an effective working relationship with their junior colleagues.

Succession Planning and Professional Development

For many years, I am embarrassed to say, we did not have much of a succession-planning strategy. However, I think that, like most organizations that hit a certain point in their history, we've had to deal with the fact that our senior leadership will turn over and retire. Consequently, we are somewhat in our infancy in thinking in a conscious and planned way about how we want to develop the next generation of leaders at Urban. We've made some efforts over the last few years, but I don't know that they've been enough.

We have always offered numerous internal learning opportunities and have made regular efforts to provide our employees with funds for professional development and external opportunities. We have always been a learning organization, so our employees have had access to many ways to further their education, including a rich tuition assistance benefit. However, learning our business is actually the high hill we have to climb. Employees have sought out courses in research methodology, advanced technical skills, and programming coursework. They've also worked hard to further their presentation and writing skills so they are well prepared for conference presentations and other more formal opportunities to disseminate their work. But courses and formal learning opportunities around such things as supervisory skills, proposal writing, budgeting, etc., are just not as well attended. I think the interest is there, but we simply don't fill the room when we host these types of formal training.

To counter this, we've begun to utilize mentoring programs as part of our talent management strategy. We have been successful over the years in attracting and retaining some of the best and brightest young people coming out of bachelor's programs in the social sciences. This success has been largely due to our culture of mentoring and growing young minds. We also help junior staff understand that professional growth will happen in a range of settings, but at some point in their careers with us, they will need to get further education in graduate school.

One of the big advantages we offer young research professionals is their first great job, which in turn will propel them to their next great job. For mid-level research staff, we are piloting an effort to partner researchers with older peers to attempt to build skill development in the "business" topics mentioned above. Because this group has probably the least amount of time to devote to formal learning programs, we're hopeful that this program will provide them with the skill development necessary to advance their careers, while providing them a "safe" place to ask questions related to not only research, but also business skills, organizational politics, and upward management. Last, for our more senior staff, we offer a culture that values work-life balance, providing good income, benefits, and security, and gives them an opportunity to mentor and learn from young talent while performing work that makes an impact.

E-learning programs have not played a major role in our institute-wide talent development process because of resource constraints. However, because our centers are pretty decentralized, and each has a dedicated stream of professional development funding, each work group has the ability to choose its own approach to e-learning and other kinds of training in areas such as programming, data analysis techniques, and more technical subjects. Therefore, some centers engage their staff members through online tools, while others do little of this sort of development.

Although HR hasn't taken the lead on many e-learning initiatives (with the exception of unlawful harassment and ethics), we have worked to encourage staff to develop non-work skills, as well. We consider all learning—professional, personal, spiritual, and emotional—vital to our employees' success at work and at life. As part of our work-life programs, we have offered our staff training in healthful eating, stress reduction, and home buying, among many other topics, and have supported and encouraged staff participation in charity initiatives ranging from food, toy, and clothing drives to the cleanup of a D.C. public school each year.

Cultural Sensitivity

Cultivating cultural sensitivity is an incredibly important area for an organization like us for a number of reasons, but here are two major reasons: (1) our international work involves going into developing countries to try to help them build better societies, and (2) our domestic policy researchers' work often focuses on poor or economically challenged communities. Often this means the communities we're working in have large minority populations, or, in the case of work abroad, the national cultures are quite different from our own. Accordingly, we need diversity in our staff to reflect many different approaches and perspectives to whatever problem we're studying, as well as appropriate levels of culture sensitivity, to be effective in our many interactions with these groups of people. Our most useful work is that which is accepted by the communities themselves because they believe we understand their circumstances.

In working overseas, therefore, we employ a number of local nationals. Of course, managing this talent presents its own unique challenges and rewards. In working with international staff, we must understand that in addition to language and cultural barriers, we are often dealing with a different talent pool regarding what motivates them. While the larger percentage of our staff (who are domestic policy researchers) have high academic backgrounds and, accordingly, are used to an academic organizational model, our people who do technical assistance work in overseas areas are more often project and program managers who often have city government backgrounds. Their formative work experiences have been in much more bureaucratic environments. And while I don't want to make too many generalizations, this group cares less than our policy researchers about theoretical explanations and much more about building a developing world. Additionally, those highly skilled professionals willing to live and work in developing and sometimes dangerous work environments are much more motivated by money and compensation packages. That's not to say that these things don't also matter to domestic staff (because they do) but there are some nuanced and some not-so-nuanced differences in these sets of values.

Measuring Success of Talent Management Strategies

Most often, we assess the success of our talent management strategies subjectively through staff feedback, exit interviews, and conversations with key personnel. However, we also measure the success of our talent management strategies by analyzing, for example, turnover. In this area, I believe the statistic that matters is attrition by level within the organization, not the global number.

Drilling down in the numbers and looking at the last ten years of data can tell me a great deal about our continued ability to attract and retain key cohorts of staff. We also look at performance appraisals every year. While we use both objective and subjective measures to evaluate performance, these can be difficult to apply without understanding the context of the ratings or how research team efforts can affect performance outcomes. Therefore, to supplement performance appraisal ratings, we also use business-oriented performance indicators measured at the individual level. For example, we look at time spent on direct research and number of project overruns. We also examine our dissemination activities. While it can be difficult to measure something like influence, external influence, and reputation, we still try to evaluate these factors. They have value, and they are what we trade on. In some ways, they are our product.

Advice for HR Executives

To cope with our changing workforces in the face of ever more aggressive competition, HR leadership cannot be reactive. Far too many people in my own profession and industry have been so. When it comes to talent management, we and they have let the world shape us, rather than try to shape our own environments. Sometimes our explanations have been lack of power or resources. However, we have great metrics and systems available to help us manage talent. We have to be more proactive in this area and take it upon ourselves to stay current, build influence in our organizations, and advance new ideas, even when it would be easier to sit idly on the sidelines.

To many of the HR professionals I've met: Please learn how to more effectively use data and apply technology. In an HR organization of our size, access to the latest technology and data analysis skills is in short supply. However, data is what HR needs. Your organization's leadership will not give you a seat at the table; you need to earn it by demonstrating that you are relevant, that you do know what's happening in your organization. If you don't have any data, you can't be relevant.

As for the generation gap, I believe it can be bridged when multiple generations communicate and collaborate. We have much to learn from each other. Although it's difficult for senior staff to admit when they don't know something, with a bit of humor and humility, information sharing is much more possible. I'll give you a personal example. A couple of weeks ago I told our Web person that I wanted to tweet a job announcement. To tell you the truth, I don't know anything about Twitter and was feeling kind of silly, old, and out-of-date. I felt comfortable asking for help, but I'm sure many others would not have. There are also situations where, especially in a think tank, there can be some hesitancy to admit you do not know something, but try it out occasionally and keep learning.

Younger employees often can teach older individuals a great deal about technology, but they also need to understand that sometimes technology isn't the answer. There is still much be said for talking to a person so you can see their reaction to what you say. What I do in HR is still called "human resources" because you have to interact with people—you still have to be able to talk to another human being.

Key Takeaways

- Talent management strategies need to address generational needs, as well as personal and professional needs.
- The organization's leaders need to take the lead in sourcing talent, developing the brand, and building compensation to retain staff because these are ultimately business decisions.
- To build collaboration and communication between departments, e-mail does not cut it. There's still nothing that takes the place of face-to-face meetings.
- To cope with changing workforces in the face of ever more aggressive competition, HR leadership cannot be reactive. These leaders need to leverage data to know what's happening in their organizations.

Deborah K. Hoover, SPHR, is currently serving as the director of human resources and a member of senior management for The Urban Institute, a Washington, D.C., policy research institution. Ms. Hoover has worked within the non-profit/academic/research sectors for many years and is an active member of the human resources (HR) professional community. She has served on the boards of the Human Resources Leadership Forum and the Washington Area Compensation and Benefits Association and participates in several other HR-related work groups in the D.C. metro area.

Ms. Hoover completed undergraduate and graduate degrees in human resources management at Ohio University and Temple University, respectively, and completed additional coursework in financial planning at Florida State University.

Integrating the Old and the New through Empowerment and Culture

Shelli Spencer, PHR
Director, Human Resources
The Hite Company

ASPATORE

Traditional HR and Talent Management

The Hite Company is a sixty-one-year old, family-owned electrical distribution company, with twenty-one locations in three states and 270 employees. Our culture and the way we manage our talent is rather traditional; we conduct performance appraisals to evaluate our employees, and then we offer performance increases based on those reviews.

As part of the appraisal, we evaluate people for succession planning to help prepare for future direction. There are general paths and training plans in place to help move people through the company. We want to determine the best people for each position, but we also need to be patient and see exactly what transpires. There is no sense in putting someone into a role for which he or she is not well suited: this is merely setting an employee up for failure.

As a family business, we are a flat organization, which translates to a limited number of upper management positions that become available. Where we may begin to see some opportunity is where many of our longest-term employees are nearing retirement now, which will allow for some upward mobility within the company. These organizational changes will help better position us strategically for growth. Our employees are very loyal, so while we can plan ahead, we do not necessarily set the plan in stone.

As the director of human resources (HR), I am responsible for managing the entire performance appraisal process, excluding the actual performance appraisals. Obviously, direct supervisors complete the appraisals. I simply manage the distribution and collecting of information. When it comes to developing our talent management strategies, the operations and sales executives become heavily involved in the process because they are familiar with where the needs are in sales, customer base, and market share. They are extremely involved in evaluating the needs, depending on growth patterns, and I serve as the go-between for the two departments, gathering information. Given that they have different goals, it is not always easy to get the two groups to listen to each other. Consequently, I step in and try to get them to evaluate the true needs of the company before we make important hiring decisions.

Staffing Trends

Over the last two years, one of the predominant staffing trends in HR, in my opinion, has been disloyalty. When the economy started to decline, the people who did not lose their jobs held onto them and were glad to have them. However, because of cutbacks, many companies found that their internal cultures were significantly deteriorating. People who were once happy simply to have a job were growing discontent and leaving.

For my company, most of the employees we have hired within the last two years were gainfully employed when they approached us about work. We have not actually had to actively recruit to fill any vacancies. A more accurate assessment is that we have had to add positions to accommodate some spontaneous growth of the company. Apparently, many of the associates who have joined us had become unhappy with their former employers. In my opinion, this speaks highly of our company's culture and reputation.

I believe it is critical to include your employees in the corporate vision and make sure that they have a sense of belonging. I'm a firm believer that when people feel comfortable, accepted, and empowered, the chance of their remaining loyal to an organization is much higher than if they are unhappy, regardless of their salary. Employees need to that they are part of the company and part of the culture. When a person does not fit in his role or in the company culture, he can taint the rest of the group. If you leave him in his position too long, he can become the rotten apple who destroys the whole barrel.

When the economy started to decline, we were forced to lay some people off, but I actually think this was beneficial to the company. We lost our most ineffective people, and we were able to truly evaluate those who remained. As a result, we were able to determine what skills and talents our employees had that weren't being put to use.

Measuring Success

We measure the success of our talent management strategies by comparing retention against turnover. I believe performance reviews can be overrated.

They are subjective, and it is difficult to extract valuable information from them. You have to believe that the evaluation process is completely unbiased, but in reality, we all know that isn't always the case. Each evaluator has a distinct point of reference from which she views the individual she is reviewing. What one person may view as acceptable work product, another may view as unacceptable. Although the expectation may, on its face and in a job description, appear clear and measurable, the result will be assessed from one of these two viewpoints.

To increase success and help our people enhance their value and improve their positions within the company, we offer e-learning opportunities. Our director of training and employee development has developed a strong electronic library in cooperation with our industry association. Furthermore, many of our suppliers have Web sites, and they offer product training that is now readily available to our employees. Not only do we encourage learning; we require it. Every employee is required to complete a certain amount of training every year as part of his or her performance appraisal. These programs have been quite successful, and the requirement aspect ensures that there is no excuse for being uninformed about a product.

The Generation Gap

The average length of employment in this company is fifteen years. Once people get past the five-year mark, they stay to become thirty-year veterans. Their comprehension is invaluable, and we have to keep them engaged so that they are willing to pass on their institutional knowledge. However, we also have to find ways to engage the younger generations. Recently, we moved from a DOS-based operating system to a Windows operating system. This has been challenging for all of our associates, but especially for some of our older employees. In this technological age, it was a necessary change that will encourage the younger generations to join our company.

Upcoming Challenges

Generally, many companies will start losing upper management through natural attrition. This is especially true in my company. As such, there is the potential for an enormous knowledge gap between the outgoing associates and the incoming ones. It will be challenging to find ways to get new college graduates to meet in the middle with long-term, experienced employees. Three generations of talent will have to co-exist and find productive ways to work together. Our HR team will have to work extra hard to make the transition peaceful and collaborative. I view HR as the mediator in every situation. We will have to "make it work."

Key Takeaways

- A loyal employee is an empowered employee. If employees are comfortable and happy, they are much more willing to stay loyal, in both good times and bad.
- Layoffs are not always a bad thing. You can eliminate your poorest performers and increase the ability and knowledge of your existing ones by pushing them into new roles and responsibilities.
- Mind the gap. The knowledge gap between generations can be enormous. Make sure long-term employees are willing to share their institutional knowledge and that incoming employees are willing to listen.

Shelli Spencer, PHR, has been in human resources in one form or another for more than twelve years. In 1992, she obtained an Associate of Arts degree in psychology from Rose State College. After working in the legal field for about six years, she earned her Bachelor of Science degree in organizational leadership in 1998 from Southern Nazarene University.

Following the achievement of her bachelor's degree, Ms. Spencer managed a small law office before becoming the director of human resources for a large, public retail music company headquartered in Oklahoma City. Since getting married and moving to Pennsylvania, she achieved her Professional in Human Resources Certification in 2007 and has now been with The Hite Company for six years.

Working Together to Create a High-Performing Organization

Daphne Logan
Senior Vice President, Human Resources
Feeding America

ASPATORE

Organization

Feeding America is the nation's leading domestic hunger-relief charity. Our mission is to feed America's hungry through a nationwide network of member food banks and engage our country in the fight to end hunger. In thirteen years, the organization has experienced many changes: branding, leadership, significant growth, and a weakened economy. Current leadership has partnered with management in our network of food banks to take the organization to new heights; we work together and know that we must be in service with this network in order to help close the "gap" on hunger in America. We have a strong network and will continue to get stronger as we act together, remain in alignment, and share best practices and knowledge. The board of directors is highly engaged and has developed organizational outcomes against which we are measured.

Talent Management Overview

Our fiscal year begins in July and serves as the kick-off to our strategic talent management timeline. We conduct organization-wide, annual performance reviews in the summer—"Performance through Outcomes and Values." This process not only determines if previous fiscal year objectives have been met ("what"), but also "how" those objectives have been achieved. Our system is merit based with additional cash awards for identified high-potential staff. Feedback happens throughout the year with the next "official" component occurring in January. We administer a "Quality of Supervision" survey to staff and use the corresponding data during midyear reviews and career development discussions in February. Shortly thereafter in March we begin succession management.

Recruitment/Retention

Feeding America aims to ensure that we have the best possible resources for recruitment and retention of talent. Even in the current economic climate, it remains a challenge to find qualified and talented individuals. When the economy improves, we are aware it may become harder to retain talent, so we are continually looking to improve our strategy. Our focus centers on the employee life cycle, which begins during the interview process. We ensure that candidates have all of the proper information and are very clear about their prospective roles, possible opportunities, and high expectations. Our turnover was 15 percent in FY10, which is considered low in the human services arena, where in some instances, it can be as high as 30 percent.

One of the most important aspects of managing talent is communication. You need to have open dialogue with staff. If you do not listen, and do not answer questions, then people will create answers and what they create may be very far from the truth. We conduct employee focus groups (on a quarterly basis) with new hires after they have been with the organization at least three months to find out how their experience has been to date: how the job/organization measures up to their expectations, and if there are any concerns or if they have ideas. We also schedule a quarterly breakfast with the CEO where employees throughout the organization can meet and chat about the organization, their work, project management, and culture.

Executive Hiring

Feeding America typically works with an executive search firm for executive positions. After final candidates have been determined, we use a consultant to conduct executive assessments that focus on leadership, cultural fit, growth potential and other critical behavioral dynamics necessary for success. When a newly hired executive joins the organization, they enter a formal integration process that is six to twelve months in length. We also offer executive coaching consultants and our board of directors has begun formal CEO succession planning. It is very important that we have plans in place to keep the organization focused on objectives during times of transition and will continue to develop internal staff who may be able to step into the CEO role if the need arises.

Supervision and Management Surveys

Each January, we ask employees a set of questions about their quality of supervision: Does my supervisor listen to my ideas and concerns; does my supervisor recognize me when I do a good job; do I work together with my supervisor to develop my skills, knowledge, and abilities to increase performance in my role? We developed a set of competencies for each area in the organization that is discussed during mid-year reviews and career development. Employees are asked to self-rate themselves against the appropriate competencies and compare against their supervisor's assessment—so they can be an active participant in their future career path. We administer an organizational health survey on an annual basis. We have scored in the 86th and 99th percentile for "workforce commitment" the last two years, respectively. Despite our high scores, we identify areas for concern and take "action planning" very seriously. One item that has surfaced more than once was around "pay." As a result, we launched an incentive plan this year for all staff. Another area we are focusing on is increased staff professional development. When we respond to survey data in meaningful ways it contributes to talent management.

Performance Management

Feeding America completely revamped our performance review system in 2008. It was coordinated by a cross-functional committee with members from various levels in the organization who presented to our executive team to gain final approval. The goal was to get input from a broad staff representation, not just the top down. One of the changes we made was to align individual objectives to organizational outcomes. It does not matter if you are an entry level professional or in senior management— what you do as an individual contributes to the overall success of the organization. Therefore, objectives must be measurable and delivered in conjunction with our values. In many organizations, people tend to focus on the "what" but not the "how." Someone who delivers 120 percent, but if "casualties" occurred along the way, they will not "Fully Meet" expectations (see chart).

Attempts to streamline the performance review process and make it easily accessible for staff are continual. All of the information is online with sections that allow both employees and managers to write notes throughout the year. The system also allows senior level staff to see how their managers have reviewed their staff and so on. This is critical because a significant part of managing talent includes a "deep dive" within each department, knowing what is taking place at all levels, not just your direct reports.

←←← Results Achieved – the "What" →→→

	Has failed to deliver the majority of results	Has delivered the majority of the expected results, but not all	(60%) Has delivered all results and may have over-delivered in some areas	Has over-delivered in most result areas or has produced extraordinary results for the organization
Exceeds the expectation for your level, against the Values/Competencies	Performance **Does Not Meet** Expectations	Performance **Fully Meets** Expectations	Performance **Fully Meets** Expectations	Performance **Exceeds** Expectations
Meets the expectation for your level, against the Values/Competencies	Performance **Does Not Meet** Expectations	Performance **Partially Meets** Expectations	Performance **Fully Meets** Expectations	Performance **Exceeds** Expectations
Is below expectation for your level, against the Values/Competencies	Performance **Does Not Meet** Expectations	Performance **Partially Meets** Expectations	Performance **Partially Meets** Expectations	Performance **Fully Meets** Expectations
	Performance **Does Not Meet** Expectations	Performance **Does Not Meet** Expectations	Performance **Partially Meets** Expectations	Performance **Partially Meets** Expectations

← Values &Competencies → The "How" (40%)

Succession Management

Succession management should not focus on the executive team exclusively; drilling down throughout the organization is prudent. We begin this process with "small round table" meetings that include directors and above by department, then vice presidents and above in the organization, and finally with the executive team who take an in-depth look at the succession plans for the entire organization. For example, in the logistics department, the VP and directors look at all of the staff in that department and discuss past and potential performance measured against future needs and strategy. The position, accomplishments, strengths, and development needs are discussed. Afterward, there are follow-up meetings to ensure that supervisors take ownership over action plans for employees defined as having growth potential. Discussions have recently started around launching a leadership academy to support talent throughout our network.

Professional Development

Feeding America values and is committed to our staff—we can't achieve our mission without a talented and mission-oriented workforce. We want to have well-rounded, experienced individuals while supporting internal career development and departmental moves. We do not usually find many accountants interested in philanthropy. We have, however, seen transitions between marketing into communication or communication into government relations. Laterals moves and promotions into other areas are career paths that illustrate how an individual can move within the organization and into senior positions. We have created career maps for certain positions ("destination roles") within the organization that show potential pathways individuals can take to reach them. Career maps are living documents and are currently being updated along with our competencies. Organizational-wide professional development opportunities are communicated to all staff through our "In the Know" calendar. Feeding America is a learning organization, striving to continually improve. We want people to enjoy their work, and be successful and recognized for their contributions while growing in their profession. When someone chooses to end employment of their own accord, hopefully, they will have meaningful experiences and "learnings" to take with them and share with others.

Key Takeaways

- Talent management starts in the first interview and continues throughout a person's employment.

- Performance should be judged not only on objectives, but how those objectives were achieved. The "how" is just as important as the "what."

- Lateral movement can be just as important as a step-up. Allow people to move around the organization to learn, utilize their skills, and grow capacity.

- Succession management should include more than just the CEO or senior staff.

- Keep staff informed, engaged (by providing resources), and aligned with the organization's strategy.

Daphne Logan is senior vice president of human resources at Feeding America, with responsibility for human resources, knowledge and learning, and administration. She has been with the organization for thirteen years. Ms. Logan has a successful record of organizational and strategic planning, using sound judgment to ensure desired business outcomes. Her expertise in talent development/management have provided sustainable resources for staff to embrace change and work collaboratively while building and maintaining productive working relationships. Previously, she was the human resources manager at Teachers Academy for Mathematics and Science. The mission of both organizations coupled with the opportunity to create and grow the human resource function led her to a career in the nonprofit sector. She is passionate about the nonprofit world and finds the sector fulfilling because she can have a positive impact (even if indirect) on the quality of life for those in need. Ms. Logan graduated from Northwestern University and has held her senior professional in human resources certification for more than ten years. She is married and lives in downtown Chicago.

Creating a Positive Culture for Long-Term Success

Debbie Hori, SPHR

Vice President, Human Resources

Bunim/Murray Productions

ASPATORE

The Elements of a Successful Talent Management Strategy

Bunim/Murray Productions is a medium-sized television production company. Our mission is to create great reality television shows. For the human resources professional, what makes this environment unique is that we have two different tiers of employees: corporate employees who work at headquarters and more temporary freelance staff who are hired and retained based on specific production needs. This second group is highly variable in number, with periods of assignment that can be as short as one day or as long as four months. Thus, the talent management strategies vary widely between these two groups.

On the production side, stringent deadlines must be adhered to in order to meet air dates, and the workload out in the field is intense. We employee hundreds of freelance employees who work for a few months during the course of that show's production; these employees leave when their short-term job is completed and often work somewhere else if we don't have another place for them. For us, it is critical that we have a system that promotes retention and/or recall of productive employees for new shows. Using an exit interview strategy consisting of an employee survey and personal interview, we have learned from our employees that even if they get a chance to earn more money working somewhere else, they choose to come back to us because of the culture. This feels like their family; it is the best place to grow; and they feel appreciated. What makes this place so special?

Our talent management strategies are an important part of our culture. These strategies can be defined as providing career advancement opportunities to promote from within the company, providing opportunities for employees at all levels to feel they are part of the bigger whole, having a kind and supportive management team, and demonstrating appreciation through various activities.

Promoting Career Advancement

Some of our executives started out in entry-level positions and have risen to the top. We hire a large number of entry-level video loggers and production assistants, and those who perform well are selected to move into other areas of production (where footage is shot) or post-production (where the final product is created). Typically, a manager will note that the employee is hard-working and capable and gets along well with others, and the manager will ask that employee questions to determine his or her area of interest and give him or her opportunities to move into that area. For example, a good crew production assistant interested in camera work who normally runs errands and makes lunch runs for the whole production team may be moved to support a particular crew and help the assistant camera operator with his tasks, thereby growing his or her skills. Non-performers don't get called back when their assignment term ends; they "self-select" themselves out naturally. The workforce is also supplemented by experienced people hired from outside the company, but it is clear to the workforce that there are plenty of opportunities for growth.

Our entry-level position for post-production is logging, where an employee types up notes of the action taking place on footage. This is a tedious job that involves sitting at a computer all day typing. However, the employees who are selected have a passion for the television industry and, specifically, for the company's popular television shows. They understand that this is their portal to more interesting job opportunities. When time permits, they are provided with short projects outside their usual job duties to give them exposure to other functions within the company and test their abilities. In exit interviews, our loggers tell us that when they work at other companies, they are sequestered in a room where they log all day, cut off from other intra-company interactions or opportunities. They tell us that compared to other companies, this is the best place to grow.

Corporate Integration: Feeling Part of the Whole

Our company strives to ensure that employees feel they contribute to and are part of the larger organization. Each month, everyone gathers for a companywide lunch, where the chairman and chief executive officer (CEO), Jon Murray, talks about each of the shows in production. His ten-minute talks are laced with humor and interesting remarks about each of the shows. Jon Murray is the co-founder of reality television, and his casual and down-to-earth remarks have the effect of binding the group into a cohesive whole. Another recurring element of these monthly lunch gatherings is recognition of significant life events within our company family. As the vice president (VP) of human resources, I personally welcome each new employee by name and recognize the recent births, marriages, and other important family events. The executive vice president of creative programming and development congratulates each employee who has a birthday in that month, and we all join in a unique happy birthday song, followed by birthday cake.

In addition to these regularly scheduled meetings, we also have company screenings for each new show. At these events, the employees gather to watch a new show shortly before it premiers and enjoy refreshments. The chairman and CEO begins the meeting by making positive comments about the show, which is followed by the executive producer thanking all of those who contributed to the show and pointing out their contributions. This serves to keep everyone informed of the variety of shows that are produced and is a great team-building event.

Personal and Corporate Kindness

People need to feel respected, appreciated, and supported to do their best work, especially in a company where creativity is an integral part of the work product. The ability to work creatively is hampered by a sarcastic or abrasive environment. Our goal is to select and retain managers who not only are talented from a business perspective, but who also treat their people well. This strategy is driven from the top of the organization. In an industry where there are tight deadlines, long hours, and sometimes extreme pressures, some managers find it difficult to control their tempers; we have found that those people are simply not a good fit for our organization. Managers who are a good fit enjoy growing the people within their work groups. The chairman and CEO treats everyone with warmth and respect, driving the culture of respect and fair treatment throughout the company. This culture builds loyalty, and the hard work and dedication needed to create a good product simply follow.

In general, the feedback we receive is that our employees return to the company time after time because of their relationships with their managers and peers. Their basic needs are met, such as having meals on time and leaving on time. Importantly, they report that their managers take great effort to make sure these basic needs are met because their managers care about them. Managers take time to thank their employees for their hard work and show their appreciation, creating a great working environment.

Creating a Caring and Appreciative Environment

We have a caring and appreciative culture, which is evident throughout all levels of the organization. Our chairman and CEO asks to meet with each intern and new corporate employee, including entry-level positions. The response to an invitation like this is amazement that such an important person would want to get to know them. This meeting reinforces that everyone is an important part of the whole and that all employees are appreciated and valued. Employee appreciation events are held every other month, which may include cookies and milk, burgers, ice cream socials, pancake breakfasts, or other events catered by popular vendors. We also have daily snack trays at 4 p.m. where employees gather to snack and socialize.

One downside of fostering a culture of kindness reveals itself when having to deal with difficult situations or underperforming employees. The management team that evolved from the culture of kindness and appreciation occasionally had a hard time initiating difficult conversations regarding performance for their underperforming employees. This dilemma was particularly apparent in the case where an employee had achieved the highest levels in their organizational area.

Two years ago, human resources started a pilot program of performance evaluations for one of our key positions. To implement this tool, the vice president of human resources interviews eight to twelve of the stakeholders in that employee's workgroup, including the direct supervisor, the management team, and the creative executives who evaluate the employee's work. Human resources developed a numerical rating and a summary of each person's performance and set recommendations on pay for performance, including eliminating increases for those who were not performing to the level expected at their pay rate, and in some cases recommending that underperforming employees not be rehired. The VP of human resources and the manager sat with the employee, providing the employee with feedback on his or her performance from the management team, pointing out areas of strength, as well as areas for improvement, and asking the employee for feedback on how his or her professional needs were being met. Being able to give an anonymous summary of performance feedback from the entire stakeholder team enabled the manager to better manage performance while retaining a supportive, kind environment. We were able to control cost for increases by tying pay to performance and provide opportunities for our best performers. This successful program has provided us with a model for future development. The goal is to expand this type of group-driven performance evaluation for other positions in the company.

Factoring Cultural Sensitivity into Talent Management Strategies

The nature of the business fortunately is helpful in encouraging acceptance of various cultures and lifestyles. Our company's work product is producing reality television shows, whose formats often involve cast members living together in a group setting. We document what happens as they interact, and edit that information into a show that tells a story. Cast members are selected for the show because of interesting characteristics, which can include a wide variety of cultural and lifestyle diversity among the cast members.

Our employees, whether they work in finance, shoot footage, capture the audio, light the set, or work in any other department, see the diversity of our cast members in situations that humanize them. We also have a diverse workforce. The first step in building cultural sensitivity is to establish common ground. We all have basic commonalities that exceed the rich variety between cultures. Having the ability to see people on television have the same day-to-day struggles we all experience, regardless of cultural, economic, or lifestyle differences, humanizes them and builds acceptance.

Our production and post-production teams get this exposure in the process of creating a television show by capturing the humanizing moments. They have exposure to cast members with a variety of races, ethnicities, sexual orientation, gender orientation, and other cultural differences. Our employees who are in support departments, such as finance, human resources, operations, and information technology, attend the show screenings along with the production and post-production teams.

Aside from the unique circumstances that are afforded to us by the type of business in which our company is engaged, our managers also attend sensitivity training led by the vice president of human resources to ensure they are well-equipped to recognize discrimination and harassment in the workplace and have the tools they need to deal with any sensitive issues that may arise.

Talent Management Challenges

Because of the nature of the business, we are unable to project staffing needs far in advance. Shows start and end within a short time, resulting in short windows to recognize and reward high achievement. Once a production budget is determined, we can start to project staffing needs, and pre-production typically starts within days of a locked budget. As a result, we are dependent on sharp-sighted and talented managers to quickly recognize their staff's skills and talents and develop those they supervise within the short time period allotted. Those managers are responsible for the quality and delivery demands of the show in addition to supervising their staff. There are many demands on their time.

When developing and implementing new strategies, it is critical to seek input from these managers to develop a program that is realistic, considering the rapidly churning workforce and production demands. Without the direct supervisor's belief in the initiative and buy-in, the implementation will not be supported and will not succeed. In this environment, human resources will be seen as an entity trying to load on more work, rather than as a partner who wants to help. We are fortunate in having a stable group of amazing managers who are open to new ideas. In developing any new talent management initiative, it is important to meet with each stakeholder and get his or her input before developing the strategy. The stakeholders will provide the best ideas for developing the program, which will maximize the chance they will take ownership of the project for a successful implementation.

Key Advice for Talent Management

There is a young, college-educated workforce that is presently having difficulty finding employment because of a sluggish economy. When the economy turns, we anticipate a surge of young workers into the workplace. This generation of new workers expects to be promoted quickly within the workforce or to be offered growth opportunities within their existing position within a short amount of time. Human resources must be poised to guide its management team to encourage development opportunities within the first year of employment to recruit and retain a competitive workforce.

Key Takeaways

- Talent management strategies are an important part of an organization's culture. These strategies encompass providing career advancement opportunities, as well as providing opportunities for all employees to feel part of the greater whole.
- Reward those employees who are hardworking and diligent, and who demonstrate initiative. They will appreciate the opportunity for growth.
- People need to feel respected, appreciated, and supported, especially in a company where creativity is an integral part of the product. Top management needs to set the tone for the organization and establish this culture so that it permeates all the way down to entry-level and freelance positions.
- When developing and implementing new strategies, it is critical to seek input from managers. Without the direct supervisor's belief in the initiative and buy-in, the implementation will not be supported and will not succeed.

Debbie Hori serves as vice president, human resources, for Bunim/Murray Productions. She oversees the human resources and recruiting functions, having joined the Bunim/Murray family in 2008. In her first year, she led the talented human resources team in process improvement initiatives, developed and delivered management training programs, and refined an infrastructure to ensure that Bunim/Murray continues to build its reputation as an employer of choice.

Bunim/Murray has a great work environment and a well-established history of developing its workforce through its grow-your-own philosophy. Bunim/Murray's successful internship program opens doors for many college students who wish to enter the